5 THINGS

with Father Bill

5 THINGS
with Father Bill

Hope, Humor,
and Help
for the Soul

WILLIAM BYRNE

LOYOLA PRESS.
A JESUIT MINISTRY
Chicago

LOYOLA PRESS.
A JESUIT MINISTRY

3441 N. Ashland Avenue
Chicago, Illinois 60657
(800) 621-1008
www.loyolapress.com

ISBN: 978-0-8294-5120-7
Library of Congress Control Number: 2020941371

Printed in the United States of America.
20 21 22 23 24 25 26 27 28 29 Lake Book 10 9 8 7 6 5 4 3 2 1

To Mom and Dad,

Thank you for showing me the joy of faith.

Contents

Foreword

By Roma Downey

I first met Fr. Bill Byrne after my husband, Mark Burnett, and I produced *The Bible* miniseries *Son of God* and *A.D.: The Bible Continues* through our company Lightworkers Media. Working with the Archdiocese of Washington, Fr. Bill produced the *Catholic Take*, a series of videos highlighting some themes and scenes from these productions that would be of interest to viewers. When I was in Washington many years ago, I invited him to lunch. There was more laughter than business served at that meal. His warmth and insights were a delight, and what started as a collaboration soon became a friendship.

Jesus once proposed that if we only had faith, we could move a mountain into the sea. Such an outrageous statement is an indication not just of the extraordinary things that people of faith can do; it also shows us that Jesus had a sense of humor. I imagine the twinkle in his eyes, as Jesus warmly invited his disciples to move closer to him and pay attention to the importance of faith.

In this delightful book, Fr. Bill follows our Lord's lead. With warmth and humor, this kind pastor helps us see how God is working in every part of our lives and how he speaks to us in our daily lives.

Our efforts at Lightworkers have a simple goal: to bring people close to God. We do this through sound and pictures, through the face and words of Jesus, through the gentle voice of his mother, through the struggles and cries of the early Church, and through the growth and flourishing of the faith. What we film with a lens we hope will find its way to people's hearts. Through family and faith-friendly movies and television, we desire to show that being a believer leads to the best way of living.

Fr. Bill does this not with cameras, actors, and music. Here he teaches us that discipleship leads to joy. Hope, humor, and help for the soul is the gift that Jesus gives us in return. Sometimes we can forget this. Thankfully, we have Fr. Bill to remind us of the importance of small acts and ways we can discover Jesus in everyday life. His insights serve as guideposts to the joy we can find when we have a little bit of faith.

Roma Downey
Producer, actress, and *New York Times*
best-selling author

A Note from the Author

Dear Reader,

"What's your favorite number?"

To this most arbitrary question asked often of kids, I always answered, "Five!" I don't know why exactly. Maybe it's because I was the fifth boy in a family of eight. Or it could be that five was my preferred number of cookies to eat. Whatever the reason, it is still my favorite number.

Some years ago, I wanted to do something a little extra special to help inspire people throughout their daily lives. I started a column in our church newspaper and returned to my old friend number five to help me do so. My short pieces followed a steady formula. I would share a short story about life and then offer five ways, suggestions, tips, or reflections on how to grow spiritually.

This book of fifty short chapters that highlight holidays and the ordinary time of day-to-day life is inspired by that idea and is offered to you as a reminder that God is never far away from you. He is in our hearts, and he is showing his love in our lives every day. I know sometimes that can be hard to believe. Life is a series of ups and downs, of joys and sorrows. Still, God is always with you, and he is always with me. I like to think that God gave us five fingers on each hand so that we could keep track of things while still holding on to what is important.

I love sports, and I love it when people give each other a high five. It means, "Hey, I celebrate you. I think you're great." This book is my high five to you. I'll hope you high five me back and that together we can grow closer to Jesus and to each other.

Love,

Fr. Bill

CHAPTER 1

Things I Learned from My Dog

My thirteen-year-old black Labrador retriever, Maggie—already blind and barely able to walk—could barely breathe one night. The next morning, I took her to her veterinarian, an almost mystical pet diagnostician named Dr. Andersen, and he discovered that she had a large tumor in her chest that was pushing against her heart. It was time, he said. I knew what he meant. My decision was difficult but right. Like all things in life, the right decision is usually the harder one.

I had named my dog Margaret Mary Byrne after the mystical nun who had visions of Jesus explaining the mysteries of his Sacred Heart. The name fit her well. She was a spiritual dog not just because she spent many hours

1

watching me pray and reciting the Rosary with me on long walks, but also because she brought out the best in all whom she met. Those who claim that dogs don't have souls never met Maggie.

In honor of my wonderful pooch, I offer you these five lessons from my dog, my beautiful friend whom I miss so:

1. Don't judge. My Maggie saw me in my most personal moments, such as collapsing on the floor after a workout or griping after a stressful encounter, throughout all my moods and all my ups and downs. She never shook her head in disgust. She just looked at me with love. She saw me for all my wonder, not my blunder. God looks at us the same way. He sees beyond our unworthiness and rejoices in our potential.

2. Forgive. If I had to go out to dinner and leave her alone, Maggie didn't slam doors when I arrived home. If my meetings went long and dinner was delayed, she wasn't passive aggressive. She was a bundle of tail-wagging-welcome-home-I-love-food furry forgiveness. Grudges get us nowhere, certainly not heaven.

3. Seek balance. Maggie loved to eat. I love to eat. Maggie loved to take walks. I need to take more walks. She forced balance upon me. It's OK to enjoy a treat as long as you get a long walk and some time to sniff the air.

4. Never complain. Toward the end of her life, Maggie was blind and her arthritis was bad. Life was not comfortable, but she never whined. To go outside, I would help her down the steps, she would sniff for the grass and plop down all with a wag in her tail. She reminded me that life is not easy, but a wagging tail is better than a whine or a growl.

5. Seek total dependence on God. I was Maggie's world. We were the best of friends. She didn't belong to a book club or worry about her Facebook page. Her concerns were the people she spent each day with, most especially me. Her devotion constantly reminded me to ask myself if I am as concerned with the happiness of my Master as Maggie was for me. I need to trust God as she trusted me. I must rejoice in the presence of the Lord as she enjoyed spending time with me. Maggie challenges me to love Jesus as much as she loved me.

CHAPTER 2

Easily Forgotten Blessings

Being a size XXL priest, I find that airline seats are usually a time of penance. In those moments, trying to nap, my body pressed up against the armrest, I pray that the next time I am in my bed, I will be extra, extra grateful for the comfort of my mattress. It works. On the rare night when I am tossing and turning, I think to myself, "I am glad I am not trying to sleep on an airplane right now." Inspired by gratitude, I usually say my prayer, and I am off to slumber land. (By the way, falling asleep while you are saying the Rosary is OK. Your guardian angel finishes it for you.)

Every day should be a time of gratitude for the blessings in our lives. Here are five blessings to keep in mind:

1. Reading. If you are able to make out these words, be grateful to your teachers and anyone else who made you learn your alphabet. Jesus is the Word made flesh, so reading is a kind of prayer, a way of interacting with the word and the Word.

2. Water. I once was lost in the Grand Canyon for a day without water. Not only did it kill any of my desire to be an avid hiker; I also learned how important water is. Not only does it keep me alive, in Baptism it promises us eternal life.

3. Unsung heroes. When the power goes out, someone climbs a pole, usually in pretty bad weather, and fixes it. If it takes longer than you expect, change your expectations. God is always trying to reach us, especially in our challenges. Be grateful for the police, firefighters, and all those who protect our freedom. Sometimes people call them angels. That's not correct. Angels are angels and people are people, different types of beings. Which brings me to . . .

4. Guardian angels. For the first moment of our existence as mere cells in our mother's womb, God decreed that a spirit, intended just for our guidance and protection, be assigned to us. We won't know how grateful we should be until we are with them around God's throne, but today begin thanking your guardian angel for helping and guiding you throughout the day.

5. Gratitude. Even our ability to be thankful is God's gift. Gratitude helps us remember that we are children of God and that all life has meaning and purpose. Being thankful should stir in our hearts the realization that Jesus died for our sins. Gratitude impels me to tell others about God and invite them to come to know how loved they are.

One final note: pray to be XXL: Extra, Extra Loving!

CHAPTER 3

Facing Terror

Jesus Christ is the Way, the Truth, and the Life. He is the Prince of Peace. Whenever I read about man-made tragedies, I think immediately how much the world needs Jesus and his church. He wants us to be the instruments of peace in the world.

After the Boston Marathon bombing, I sat glued to the television watching the terror, the manhunt, and the arrest of the suspects. I was proud of Boston and our country for our bravery and vigilance. While violence may be needed to stop a villain, it is not the only or the best tool in our arsenal. In the long run, the Gospel is the only way to true peace in our world. Poison is never the antidote to poison. Love must be the victor, and as followers of Jesus we must make sure that we lead the way. So, I offer five ways to face terror:

1. Teach kids about Jesus. Babies are not born with hate; they learn it. If our education system devolves into a place where truth is replaced by opinion, we need faith-based education more than ever. It is one thing to tell children to be nice to one another; it is much better to teach them that we are all children of a loving God, instilling a love for all of creation. Catholic schools, religious education programs, and churches do this. Do what you can to support faith-based education.

2. Slow down. The prayer Jesus taught us has it all. In just a few sentences, the Lord's Prayer leads us through honor, worship, aligning ourselves to God, and asking for mercy, while acknowledging our need for forgiveness. The beauty of such prayers is that they become a part of us like our breathing or our heartbeat. The challenge is that we can often recite them without being conscious of what we are saying to God. On a walk or on your knees, in the car or in a pew, take some time to say your favorite prayers together slowly. Stop and chat about a phrase. Like a deep, slow breath, a deep, slow prayer brings life.

3. Eat dinner together. Our Lord gave us the greatest gift of his love in the Eucharist at the Last Supper. As Vatican Council II taught us, the family is the domestic church, the most localized version of the Body of Christ. Each meal, with a blessing at the beginning, can be a chance to experience Christ's love. For parents, the dinner table is an altar where God's love is shared. Dinner is a chance to ask how things are going with our family and our friends and to actually find the answer. The food does not have to be good for the love to be great. Terror cannot enter a family if the bond of caring is strong enough to keep it out.

4. Be a peacemaker. At the end of Mass when the priest or deacon says, "Go in peace," he is telling us to bring the Eucharistic Lord out to the world in our person. The world needs Christ, and Christ asks us to carry him out to the world. Holiness is not really going to Mass; it is leaving from the Mass to bring Christ to others. Go out and bring peace to others.

5. Be the light of Christ. Darkness is the absence of light. Sin is the absence of good. If we want to stop the dark, we must be the light. If we want to end terror, we must be the love of Christ to the world—and that means even around the watercooler when the gossip starts.

CHAPTER 4

Things We Shouldn't Forget to Do

I once had to throw out the first pitch at a local community baseball game. A group of priest friends were there, and it had been twenty years since I had pitched a baseball. Even back in my high school days, I was no Cy Young, so I was very nervous that I would either throw the ball into the dirt or toss it over the catcher's head and crown the hot dog guy.

I spent all week practicing my pitching skills and, upon reflection, I regretted that it had been twenty years since I actually tossed a ball around. Life is too short not to play some catch. So today, I offer five things we shouldn't forget to do:

1. Call an old friend. I recently reconnected with an old pal from seminary. He had ended up in the hospital, and I decided to call to wish him well. It took no time at all to reconnect. From experience, I know that an email, a note in the mail, a text, or an actual phone call is not as awkward as it may seem at first. If someone doesn't respond, just know that you tried and did the right thing.

2. Lie on the ground and look at the clouds. God is an amazing artist. Not only can he paint the sky, he can change it constantly. Take a few moments to decompress by staring into the blue (or gray if it's a cloudy day). It's also a good idea to remind yourself every so often just how big his sky is so that we can remember how small his earth is too. Keep things in perspective.

3. Be quiet. This is the hardest of all because we have so much noise in our worlds. Even my refrigerator beeps at me when I leave the door open. The quietest place of all is a church in the middle of the day. Pay a visit. Sink into the silence like you would a hot tub. No need to say anything, God knows it already. Well, I guess you could say, "Thank you."

4. Do a divine two-step. One of my favorite scenes in Scripture takes place in 2 Samuel 6. As the Ark of the Covenant is being carried into Jerusalem, the great King David precedes it, dancing with joy. His wife and others criticize him, but he doesn't care. David is proud to rejoice in God. Pray to be free enough to please God and to not worry about what others think.

5. Smell the roses. Literally stop and smell some roses. If you live in the city and there are no roses to be found, stop at a drugstore or department store and sniff some perfume or cologne. Just remember that there is more to the world than we normally observe—or smell.

CHAPTER 5

Fight the Good Fight

A lot of bad things have happened in my neighborhood of Capitol Hill in Washington, D.C. Some years ago, the shootings at the Navy Yard left us shaken and sad. A mentally ill woman tried to ram the gates of the White House and led police on a chase with her toddler in the back seat, endangering many lives. She was killed by police. A man lit himself on fire on the National Mall. He died, and no one knew his name. On top of it all, the shutdown of the world because of the coronavirus pandemic has left many of my parishioners confused and worried. It's all pretty scary stuff.

God does not make bad things happen. We live in a world that has been wounded in many ways by our forgetting of God. The power of the Gospel message is that God never forgets us. When bad things happen, God will *always* bring good from bad. The Jesus story didn't end on Calvary; it continues throughout history in the resurrected Christ. Jesus always wins, and his kingdom is eternal!

For us, the kingdom comes when we align ourselves with God by bringing him into our lives in an even deeper and more committed way. In doing this, we fight the battle of life with the strongest weapons of all: faith, hope, and love. Here are five ways to fight the good fight:

1. Create a house of prayer. When we think of the most basic level of the church, most often we picture our local parish, but Vatican II told us that the home is this first building block of the kingdom. The fathers of Vatican II called the home the "domestic church." Make your house, apartment, condo, or dorm room a place where Christ is welcome and comfortable. Always practice humility and forgiveness. Sweep out anything that is not worthy of the King's residence. Saying "I am sorry" keeps a home beautiful.

2. Take a minute. The Morning Offering should become a common spiritual practice. When you open your eyes, thank God for the gift of the day. Offer the day back to him, and ask yourself to be an instrument of his peace. Try to recall that offering throughout the day.

3. Recall. If you are trying to remember something, write it down. Put a note at your desk or in your calendar that says, "Remember!" Powerful things happen when we intentionally remember them.

4. Savor the in-between. Much of our day is filled with the "in between" or the "not yet." We wait in line, sit in traffic, drum our thumbs waiting for someone to show up. These times should not be drudgery but opportunity. Fill them with prayer. Keep a list handy of the people you know who need prayer the most. (I keep my list on my phone.) Sitting in the doctor's office, put the magazine down and lift up your soul.

5. Recognize the last minute. As you are going to bed, thank God for the day. Replay the mental video of your day and recall where God was and where you might not have been there to meet him. Make a plan for the next day to build on the graces of that day. When you wake up the next morning, your offering is the plan from the night before.

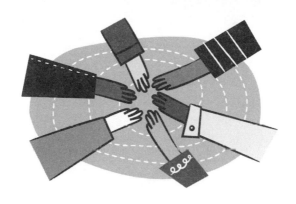

CHAPTER 6

Ways We Can Live Together as Children of God

We cause a lot of trouble in our world. Racism is a sin, an ugly devaluation of God's creativity. It lessens us in every way, most particularly because it inevitably leads to violence and death. In order to find the cure, we have first to study the wound. Then we can turn to the Divine Physician for healing. So, here are five ways we can live together as children of God. Let's start in the Garden of Eden:

1. Embrace your family. Notice that Genesis does not say, God created us white or black or any color. While God is indeed one, his creation reflects the unlimited complexity of his glory and wisdom. Much of Christian art has pictured

God as an old white guy, and somehow Jesus got blue eyes. While I am not suggesting that this is the cause of racism, these human images of the divine do limit God's universality. When God was creating the world and sky and sun in his infinite wisdom, he knew your name. He was calling each of us into being at the proper time as part of his plan. We are all children of God, which means we are all brothers and sisters. Never forget that. We are one family.

2. Know who you are. In order for us to be friends, you have to be you and I have to be me. Any deception destroys the relationship. So, for us to be friends with God, we must recognize him as the *only* God and joyfully accept our being his creatures. When the Devil tempts Adam and Eve with the juicy fruit of being like gods, he is tempting them away from being themselves. Poof. There went any chance of a complete and whole loving relationship with God. Jesus, however, reminds us to love our neighbor as ourselves and in the process, we grow closer and closer to who we really are, God's creation. Rejoice in being a creature, not a creator. Also, if it's between believing a snake or God, believe God!

3. Shift your focus. As soon as Adam and Eve broke their relationship with God, shame entered human experience.

Once we are disconnected from God and we forget that we are his children, we begin to hate ourselves. If I can hate myself, then I can definitely hate you. Mix that with trying to be gods, and you have people deciding that other people should no longer exist. Servant of God Dorothy Day wrote, "I really only love God as much as I love the person I love the least." Reflect on the people you love least and discover where you need to let God's love flow more fully through you to them.

4. Will the good for the other. This is Adam's response when God asks him if he ate the forbidden fruit. This is when the wimp came into existence. He throws Eve right under the bus, or maybe it was a hippopotamus since buses didn't exist yet. We have to own our sins not blame others. When Jesus says to love our enemies, he did not say that our enemies had to become pleasant chums in order for this to happen. To love is to will the good of the other. The good is what God knows is best for them. To end racism, we must first acknowledge our own biases, annoyances, hates, our own sins. Then we must *beg* God to turn those feelings into a desire to will the good for the other.

5. Fall in love. St. John penned these words: "God so loved the world." In other words, God loves the whole world, not just part of the world or some people in the world. Jesus died for those who praised him and the people who spat on him. The secret to unlocking this kind of love in ourselves is not just to follow Jesus but to fall in love with him. In that love we find that we are all children of a loving Father who has a plan for us all. Then, we stop believing the snake who always lies. That's how we end the sin of racism.

CHAPTER 7

Declutter

Decluttering is a time to clean out the cobwebs, air out the rooms, and freshen things up. This activity isn't just great for organizing your home; it works great for your soul, too. Why not do both at the same time? Here are five ideas for year-round springlike cleaning:

1. Organize your closet. If you have not worn an item of clothing for a year, you probably won't ever. Take a few items, get them cleaned, and donate them to a local charity or someone you know who might need them.

2. Offer it up. What is your least favorite chore? Doing the dishes? Mowing the lawn? Pick a particular intention:

a sick friend, a lonely family member, someone who died. Now offer your misery for that intention as you do your least favorite chore. What was annoying will now be an act of love.

3. Put away clothes. As you pack the gloves and hats away for the summer or put the shorts and Hawaiian shirts into storage for winter, make a spiritual plan. How about reading one of the Gospels? Pick one and read a little bit each day and open your heart to meeting Jesus in a new way. He has some stuff to say to you.

4. Get rid of old junk. Even more satisfying than dragging stuff to the curb is dropping sins off in the box. Go to confession. Reconciliation is not just for Advent and Lent.

5. Weed the garden. Do you have a few pesky sins that keep popping up in life? Find your calendar and begin a month of freedom. Pick the main weed and decide to pull it by the end of the month. Mark the calendar each day. Don't be discouraged if you have a bad day. It will take some work and some time, but it's worth it. If the repeat offender shows up again, put twenty dollars each time in a jar, and about eighty dollars from now you should be free. Use the money for a special treat to celebrate pulling that weed.

CHAPTER 8

Remembrance

I recall as a little boy watching the television while the Vietnam draft lotteries were being announced. I did not understand it, but I knew my mom and dad were worried. The youngest of eight children, I had brothers who were draft age. Neither of my brothers was drafted, and my family was spared the pain of seeing the men they love leave to fight that war. My sister, a surgeon and a religious sister, served in Afghanistan, but thankfully she returned home to continue her service to the poor in Washington, D.C.

For many families, the story is much different. I am grateful that my family did not have to suffer the tragedy of losing a son or a daughter to war, but I am grateful to the families who did. We are a nation of heroes. Memorial

Day is our nation's opportunity to pause and remember the sacrifices made by so many so that freedom and democracy may be preserved both at home and abroad.

With war often so far away, it's easy to forget how important it is to remember. Memorial Day marks more than the beginning of summer. Amidst the trips to the beach and the joy of cookouts, we cannot forget our fallen heroes and our living warriors who bore the burden of battle so that we can live free. With a grateful heart, I offer you five ways to not forget on Memorial Day and to keep Memorial Day every day in your heart:

1. Give a minute. In May 2000, President Clinton asked that we stop each Memorial Day at 3 p.m. for a national moment of remembrance. For Catholics, 3 p.m. is the hour of mercy, a daily time to reflect on Jesus' death on the Cross. Our moment of remembrance should be a time to commend those brave souls to the love of Christ for all eternity.

2. Say a cookout prayer. When you are enjoying the day off and grilling the hot dogs and burgers, don't forget to say grace before digging in. Ask everyone to say a Hail Mary for all our dead and for our veterans who today suffer the wounds of war.

3. Put your flag out. This is something I often forget, but it's important to remember that we are the "home of the brave." Each star and stripe on our flag is a reminder of all the good men and women who courageously helped to build our nation.

4. Tell the story. We cannot remember what we never learned. It would be sad if our young people only get their information from a website. Every family has its own heroes; you may be one of them. Find time to share and ask for the tales of your heroes. Remembering is not just recalling a story; it's sharing it and passing it down through generations.

5. Have a Mass said. The best for last: There is no greater gift for the living or the dead than to have a Mass offered for them. The grace of the sacrifice of the Mass is applied to the soul of another. Simply stop by the parish, make the customary offering, and a Mass will be scheduled for your hero, your veteran, or your fallen warrior. Celebrate Memorial Day with the words, "Do this in remembrance of me."

CHAPTER 9

Prayers for Our Nation

My parish, St. Peter's on Capitol Hill in Washington, D.C., includes the House of Representatives. After each election, we host a prayer service for the members before they take their oath of office. Our congresswomen and -men of many faiths stand together in prayer for our nation and for one another. Like the inauguration of the president, it is a marvel to see that the democratic experiment conceived by our founders is working, albeit imperfectly.

Catholicism is neither red nor blue, but the teachings of the church are always true. Regardless of how we might have voted, after the election we must unite in prayer for our nation, so that we don't lose sight of the duty that is ours as Americans and Catholics. I offer you five prayers for our nation:

1. For life. We witness so much violence each day when we pick up the newspaper or watch the television. Our hearts are hardened by so many years where a culture of death has prevailed. We cannot be surprised by the violence against the young when the sin of abortion for the entire term of the pregnancy is still permitted. Lord, give us the courage to stand up and fight for life, for you, in the unborn.

2. For the poor. As the economy rises and falls, we have all felt the struggle; those at the bottom, however, feel it the hardest. Elected officials have to make budget decisions. The key to helping the poor is not just a sandwich today, but also a job tomorrow. Lord, help our leaders think beyond immediate solutions for the poor, and guide them to seek sound and long-range resolutions to poverty.

3. For families. Marriage between a man and a woman is a gift from God, intended from the creation of humankind for the gift of children and the building up of society. Lord, guide couples to know that you are the source of their love so that husbands and wives may realize their dignity and their duty. May they always be open to life, and may the world see in their love how dearly you love us all.

4. For veterans. Many of our men and women return from the wars with both visible and invisible scars. They are heroes. Our nation cannot forget this fact. Lord, help me to remember that the war is ongoing, the wounds are real, and the men and women who serve sacrifice much. Help me to reach out with arms of gratitude and welcome to those who return. Let our nation not forget its obligation to those who have fought for freedom.

5. For religious freedom. As the First Amendment states, "Congress shall make no law respecting an establishment of religion, or prohibiting the free exercise thereof . . ." Lord, you have given us the gift of freedom: the choice to worship you or not, to serve you, or to walk away. This freedom is a gift from you, not from any civil authority. Please grant our nation a deep respect for the conscience of all men and women. Give us the wisdom to recognize when that freedom is threatened, and the courage to stand up for the rights that only you can bestow.

Amen.

The *Delightful* Mysteries of the Rosary

I am not pretending to be St. John Paul II, who gave us the Luminous Mysteries, but I have come up with my own set of mysteries in honor of Mary's day-to-day life. I wish that I could claim that I received these in a mystical state; rather, these are the result of my own mental wanderings as I have prayed with the beads.

Although the Gospels don't explicitly say that Mary smiled, we know that she must have since she is a human like you and me. I have chosen times in the life of our Lady and our Lord Jesus when she must have cracked a smile. While I don't expect Pope Francis to adopt these for the universal church, perhaps you may enjoy my five Delightful Mysteries of the rosary:

1. Jesus gets unusual baby gifts. As the Magi laid down the gold, frankincense, and myrrh, I imagine Mary's smile of gratitude mixed with an interior giggle. I imagine her thinking, "These guys know nothing about a newborn." Frankincense, an expensive incense or perfume, and myrrh, an anointing oil, have symbolic significance, but they are not particularly practical when you need diapers. Joseph must have been glad for the gold when they had to head to Egypt. Mary teaches us to be gracious with those who might not know better.

2. Mary attends Jesus' soccer game. The Delightful Mysteries can include anything imaginable in the life of the Holy Family from the time that Jesus was twelve, when he was found in the temple, until he began his public ministry at the age of thirty. These eighteen years are called the "hidden life" because Scripture does not record any of the events. It was then that Jesus was growing up and learning from Mary and Joseph how to be a man. Other names for this mystery might be "Mary hosts a kid's birthday party" or "Mary and Joseph wait up for the kids to get back from prom." You are limited only by your imagination. What's important is that the hidden life is really a mirror of your own life.

3. Mary waits outside. In Matthew 12, Jesus addresses a crowd and is told that his mother and brothers are outside. He says to his listeners, "Who is my mother? Who are my brothers?" And stretching out his hand toward his disciples, he said, "Here are my mother and my brothers. For whoever does the will of my heavenly Father is my brother, and sister, and mother" (Matt. 12:48–50). Mary might have been annoyed, but I picture a big smile as she rejoiced that the love of Jesus was not limited to his mother but had no limits. It includes even you and me.

4. Mary meets the resurrected Jesus. Scripture does not record this moment, but it does not take much to imagine the smile on Mary's face as not only her Savior but also her son is alive. Feel her joy.

5. Mary receives the Eucharist. Jesus is truly present in the Most Blessed Sacrament in his body, blood, soul, and divinity. As truly as Mary carried him in her body after the Annunciation so also do we carry the same Jesus truly present in our bodies as we receive him at Mass. Imagine our Lady's sublime joy and her big smile when she experiences that intimacy with her boy Jesus, her Lord, again at each Mass. That smile must be illuminating!

CHAPTER 11

Myths of Sainthood

As brushes with greatness go, I have had a couple. I saw President George W. Bush drive by when I was walking my dog, and I once saw the Washington Wizards cheerleaders warming up on the National Mall before the National Cherry Blossom Festival parade. I actually wasn't attending the parade. Again, I was walking my dog and was frankly annoyed by the crowd of men on the sidewalk until I realized whom the men were looking at.

I once shook the hand of St. John Paul II. I was a seminarian and in a group that was granted an audience. As he passed and I fumbled to kiss his ring, I spoke these memorable words, "Hello Father Holy," and finished the sentence with several lines of gibberish. I met a saint in the making, which is actually something I think I do a lot when I talk to my parishioners.

Some people feel that the way to become a saint is just to die, as if a life of heroic virtue means nothing. (Purgatory is whole different topic, but it's a good one.) So, perhaps it's time to clear up some misunderstanding with five myths of sainthood:

1. Popes don't "make" saints. The pope cannot make a saint. Rather he solemnly declares someone to be among those who are models and intercessors for the whole church. He recognizes them to be in heaven either because they were martyrs or lived lives of heroic virtue.

2. Catholics don't worship saints. Anyone who says that either does not know what they are talking about or is a liar. There: I said it, and I mean it. We give God alone glory and adoration. We honor saints for the way they have lived their lives devoted to Jesus. We should honor people who do good things, not because they need it, but because it teaches the rest of us how to be better.

3. Saints aren't middlemen and -women. Why do we need a middleman when we can just go straight to Jesus? Jesus is our one mediator—but not our sole intercessor. If I have a special need, I would not think twice about asking a friend to pray for me. My friends help me carry my load to the one who can help me unburden it. In the book of Revelation, we hear that before the throne of God there are "gold bowls filled with incense, which are the prayers of the saints" (Rev. 5:8). Why not have the holy ones fill their bowls with your prayers?

4. It's not that God doesn't answer. "I prayed and nothing happened." When nothing happens, it does not mean that the saints were asleep at the wheel or that God doesn't care. God never says no. He says, "I have something better." Pray to gain trust in his will.

5. Saints aren't superheroes with magical powers. Many people think that saints are different than us ordinary humans, as if they had magical powers on earth. No! They were people like you and me who just tried really hard to trust in Christ and let his love flow through them. They *are* superheroes, but their special powers were faith, hope, and love. These powers are available to us all the time, which is why Jesus calls *all* of us to be saints.

CHAPTER 12

The Sacred Heart

If you had a May wedding, the bridesmaids wore blue. If you had a June wedding, the bridesmaids wore red. Such was the custom not so long ago for Catholic nuptials. Blue was to honor the Blessed Mother and red to honor the Sacred Heart of Jesus. While most modern couples have never heard of such devotions, some brides and grooms will still bring flowers to our Mother at their weddings. Many parishes continue to crown the statue of our Lady in May and have communal Rosaries. I think the Sacred Heart of Jesus has faded a bit from Catholic consciousness. I know it's not a competition, but I think it's time for the Sacred Heart of Jesus to get the attention it deserves.

Devotion to the Sacred Heart of Jesus, a human heart that is inflamed with divine love, is a powerful meditation that helps us understand who Jesus is and how much he loves us. I think it is time for us as human beings, seekers, and believers to renew our devotion, and so I offer you five ways to reflect on the Sacred Heart of Jesus:

1. A sacred sonogram. Imagine if sonograms had existed at the time of Jesus. Just a little more than a week after the Annunciation, when Mary said yes to becoming the mother of God, we would have seen something amazing on that screen, a little beating heart. That tiny pulse, undetectable to the human ear but resounding in heaven, meant that our God has a heart.

2. What John didn't hear, but the angels did. At the Last Supper, John the Beloved laid his head on Jesus' chest. Jesus knew that Judas, one of his chosen apostles, was going to betray him. What John did not hear but again echoed in heaven was the sound of a breaking heart. The Sacred Heart is as human as yours and mine. It is a sign of the true humanity of Jesus. His heart quickened when he laughed with a loved one, and it ached with sorrow when he experienced betrayal. Think how truly his heart feels your joys and sorrows.

3. See blessings, not bitterness. "But when they came to Jesus and saw that he was already dead, they did not break his legs, but one soldier thrust his lance into his side, and immediately blood and water flowed out" (John 19:33–34). The Sacred Heart of Jesus was wounded and from that wound came blood and water. From his suffering, blessings flowed, the waters of Baptism and the blood of the Eucharist. From our pains and hurts, what flows? Grudges, blame, and anger? Or mercy, compassion, and forgiveness? Don't wait for suffering before you turn to Christ on the Cross, but begin to pray now so that when you are put to the test, blessings and not bitterness will flow from your wounded side.

4. Some wounds never heal. When the soldier thrust the lance into Jesus' side, he was already dead. As Thomas learned, those wounds never healed. He was able to feel the marks of the crucifixion and put his hand into Jesus' side. The water and blood, Baptism and Eucharist, have never ceased to flow from the side of Christ. His mercy is without end. After you receive Communion at Mass, stay a few minutes and recall his overwhelming, never-ending generosity. Pray that just as his love flows from the Cross into you and me, that love may flow from you and me into the world.

5. Like unto thine. The Sacred Heart of Jesus, a human heart, opened the gates of heaven for each of us. In Jesus, humanity entered into union with God that could only happen when God became a man. As he took a human heart, he invites us into his divinity. When you think of the Sacred Heart, pray this invocation, old and yet so new:

Jesus, meek and humble of heart,
make my heart like unto Thine.
Heart of Jesus, burning with love for me,
inflame my heart with love of Thee.
Amen.

CHAPTER 13

Guardian Angels

Some time ago, I had promised to visit an elderly religious sister. My day started. I got busy and then distracted. As I was rushing to another appointment, I suddenly remembered, "Don't forget Sister Marta." As I turned my car around to go to her convent, I said a prayer of thanks to my guardian angel for reminding me to keep my promises.

October 2 is the day we stop and remember what the psalms proclaim: "He commands his angels with regard to you, to guard you wherever you go" (Ps. 91:11). We each have a guardian angel given to us to by Christ for watchful care and intercession.

The *Catechism of the Catholic Church* explains that "[t]he angels surround Christ their Lord. They serve him especially in the accomplishment of his saving mission to men" (*CCC* 351). The word *angel* means one who is sent, so, as St. Augustine explains, *angel* is not what they are but what they do. They are pure and personal spirits who have intelligence and will, and God has given us each such a messenger to help us out. In honor of these amazing gifts from God, I offer you five things to remember about guardian angels:

1. Sweat the small stuff. God is not a faraway, abstract, disinterested God. He cares about and works through the smallest details of our lives. We can turn to our angels with the little stresses in our day. We can ask them for guidance in a traffic jam or a logjam or when we are tempted to eat too much jam. In these small, private moments we can learn a great deal about how dearly loved we are.

2. Seek great examples. St. Thomas Aquinas once wrote in his *Summa theologica* that "angels work together for the benefit of us all." Try making this the special prayer you make when others around you are getting on your nerves: *Help me, Lord, to work with others for the good of all your people.*

3. Better than texting. When I can't find someone whom I need to speak to, I ask my guardian angel to ask this person's guardian angel to tell him or her I would like to talk to them. I routinely do this when I need to talk to someone in my family and they're busy. It works!

4. Turn their receivers on. Suggestion 3 works best when others are aware that they have a guardian angel so talk them up. Remind people to pray to their angels, to turn to them. Don't be afraid to tell others of the times when your special spirit has helped you.

5. They're real. Those special nudges you get—the missed accident, the call you make just at the perfect time—these are the workings of God in your life through his angels. In their honor and for their intercession, pray this classic prayer regularly:

Angel of God, my guardian dear,
to whom God's love commits me here,
ever this day, be at my side,
to light and guard, to rule and guide.
Amen.

CHAPTER 14

The Immaculate Conception

The Immaculate Conception is often misunderstood. It refers not to Jesus' conception but his mother's conception in the womb of her mother, Anne. As a matter of biology and mathematics, nine months is the gestation time for a human baby. December 8 is nine months before Mary's birthday on September 8, while the Annunciation, Jesus' conception when the angel Gabriel visits Mary, is March 25, nine months before Christmas. See, it all works out. Even though it's often misunderstood, the Immaculate Conception makes a big difference for you and me. So, to honor Mary and to explain our destiny, I offer you five reasons the Immaculate Conception is really important:

1. It's about me. While the teachings about Mary, like her Immaculate Conception and her Assumption into heaven, tell us about her, we celebrate these things because they are also about us. Mary is not just Jesus' mother; she is also his first disciple, so she is constantly leading us to him. Mary was conceived without the stain of Original Sin and therefore the worthy vessel to receive and nurture the Son of God. She prefigures our own Baptism. We are washed clean of Original Sin so that God can come live in us.

2. He dwells in us. Preserved from Original Sin, Mary is able to say yes to the angel Gabriel when he announces God's plan that she should be the mother of his Son. Again, she paves the way. Just as truly as Mary had Jesus in her body, so too do we when we receive Jesus in communion in his body, blood, soul, and divinity.

3. But I mess up. Although Mary never sinned, she still points the way for us. While Jesus hung upon the Cross, all of his friends except for Mary, John, and a few others ran for the hills. Mary stood at the foot of the Cross in complete trust. She says to us that even though we may falter, we need to stay close to Jesus. He gave us his mercy in the sacraments to do just that. When things get hard, don't run away from him; run to him.

4. It can be really scary. Following Jesus means being willing to hand over our own opinions and plans to let his plan, the only true way for us to be happy, be our real way of life. This can be really scary, especially when we don't know what will happen. One of the first things Mary and Joseph do after the birth of Jesus is present him in the temple. They give back to God what God has given to them. Simeon in the temple tells Mary at that moment, "*You yourself a sword will pierce,*" predicting the sorrow she will experience (Luke 2:35). Yet, she always trusts in God and asks us to do the same.

5. Where's this headed? Finally, at the last moments of her life on earth, Mary is carried body and soul to heaven. She experiences the truth that we profess each week at Mass, "the resurrection of the dead and the life of the world to come." Mary's Immaculate Conception made it possible for her to bear the Lord and so for us to bear the Lord. She who bore the Word was born by the angels to heaven. There she constantly draws us closer to him so that we may one day through Christ's mercy join her as saints in heaven. Now that's really important!

CHAPTER 15

Be Glad for Purgatory

November is the month of saints and souls. We begin with the feast of All Saints, celebrating all those who have made it to heaven, both the famous and the unknown. We ask them to pray for us that someday we will enjoy the fulfillment of all our hopes and dreams with God for eternity. The rest of the month we pray for the souls in Purgatory. The *Catechism of the Catholic Church* explains, "All who die in God's grace and friendship, but still imperfectly purified, are indeed assured of their eternal salvation; but after death they undergo purification, so as to achieve the holiness necessary to enter the joy of heaven" (*CCC* 1030). What does this mean?

Imagine if Mother Teresa and I were riding a tandem bike around town. Suddenly, a tourist bus careens out of control and smashes into us. We both die, but did we both die in the same state of grace? I don't think so. She, as her canonization now shows, was definitely ready. I am no Mother Teresa, and I pray that I may be given a chance to be purified of things that hold me back and so be made ready to enter into heaven. If God in his goodness did not give me this chance, if I had to be completely ready when I die, the other option is very bad. We need to pray that each of us goes to heaven and live with that in mind. So, with a grateful and hopeful heart, I offer you five reasons to be glad for Purgatory:

1. Heaven is a no-grudge zone. You can't bring your grudges in, and neither can anyone else. Purgatory moves us beyond the past and into the eternal love of God. How freeing!

2. You cannot cross over to the other side of Glory Boulevard. St. Paul, before his conversion when he was known as Saul, participated in the murder of St. Stephen. Now they are both saints, bonded in the love of God forever. They can't avoid each other but since God's forgiveness reigns in them, they don't want to. The terrible stuff does not come with us, only the healing and forgiveness.

3. I still cringe when I remember what I did. Think of those terrible things we have all done. I keep them hidden in my heart and still cringe when I remember them. God's love scrubs them away. Remember, you don't have to wait for Purgatory to begin that process.

4. It's hard, but it's good. All the good stuff in life usually comes from sacrifice. Health comes from closing the fridge and strapping on your jogging shoes. Great ideas come from reading, studying, and paying attention. Babies, well ask any mom! Purgatory is not going to be easy, but it is right. Cleaning wounds can hurt, but the healing is worth the sacrifice.

5. It's easier if you start now. We don't need to wait for the final tally to begin the healing, the amends, the letting go. Jesus teaches us to love our enemies. Love means willing the good of the other without expecting anything in return. When we will the good for another, we are asking God to give them what he knows they need, not what we want them to have. This may be justice, mercy, healing, or forgiveness.

CHAPTER 16

Vacation Musts

You're going on a road trip. The minivan is loaded with swim fins and snorkels or snow skis and mittens. Did you forget anything? Make sure you have a checklist of things not to forget before going on vacation:

1. Download the Mass schedule. Unless you are vacationing in Saudi Arabia, there will likely be a Catholic church where you are going. Take a few minutes to search the internet for Mass times. If you wait until you get there, it might be too late.

2. Give back. Traveling can be expensive. However, take a second to remember that there are loads of people who have no chance of getting away to the beach or the mountains. Donate and drop some extra cash into the poor box as a way of showing gratitude for the blessings of time away.

3. Be artsy. Hopefully, you have a crucifix on your wall and a statue of the Blessed Mother in your house. Sacred art helps remind us of how dearly we are loved by our Savior. Take a little sacred art with you on vacation so that you don't go on vacation from God. Put a holy card by the mirror in the bathroom and a small crucifix or rosary next to the bed. It is simple, but it makes a big difference.

4. Remember your envelopes. As a pastor, I have an important reminder. You may go on vacation, but the electric company doesn't (which is a good thing). You will make your priest smile, because when the collection goes down, the air conditioning or heating bill usually goes up.

5. Say a car prayer. "Jesus, Mary, and Joseph, protect us on our way." Invite the holy family along for the ride.

CHAPTER 17

Tips for "Sonbathing"

I don't tan. My skin was designed for Cork, Ireland, not the Caribbean. My complexion ranges from white to red to peeling (depending on how long I am in the sun). I am usually a walking pile of sunblock covered in a big hat. While I caution everyone to stay out of the sun, I am a strong advocate for catching some of the Son's rays. Jesus is the Way, the Truth, and the Life, and if we don't get enough time with him, we can get lost, begin to believe lies, and feel less alive. This summer I strongly encourage you to catch some of his rays with my five tips for "Sonbathing":

1. Seek direct exposure. Long-distance relationships are hard to maintain. Real love requires face time. At Mass on

Sunday, we have the deepest encounter with the Lord in the Eucharist. If you can make a weekday Mass, that is a wonderful way to allow the Lord more deeply into your week. If you can't go to a daily Mass, try to stop by a church and visit Jesus in the tabernacle at least once a week. Call the most convenient parishes and see when they are open for prayer. If they're locked, come to St. Peter's on Capitol Hill; we're open every day, all day.

2. Find a good reflector. To ensure an even tone, some people put some tinfoil on cardboard to reflect the rays so that their jaw is as equally exposed as their nose. The strongest rays of the Son come from the Scriptures and the sacraments, but Christ speaks to us in many ways. Pope Francis has emphasized to the church that we need to have a heart for the poor. In serving others we serve Christ not just metaphorically; we also truly encounter Jesus in the poor. Those in need are powerful reflectors of the Son.

3. Multitask. The good news is that we can get the Son all through our day. It does not just have to happen in church. Our commute, waiting in the dentist's office, in line at the bank, on hold on the phone: all of these are perfect chances for multitasking. Have a favorite prayer handy, and instead of being bored, be blessed.

4. Avoid "Sonblock." I am not talking about S-P-F; I am talking about S-I-N. God does not force us to love him. He invites us gently. Sin disrupts our capacity to hear him and experience his love most fully. Seeking his forgiveness is not just for Advent and Lent. Let the light in every day.

5. Glare is good. Normally, we avoid glare, but glare from the Son is good. Not only is it good, it is essential to effective Sonbathing. Good gifts get better when we share them. Be God's glare. Let his love continually reflect off of you and into the darkness of our world. I believe the most effective tool for evangelization is joy. A smile is the best way to win hearts for Christ, and a smile is the surest sign of an avid Sonbather.

CHAPTER 18

Suggestions for Spiritual Reading

I love a good book, and often I carry more than one with me. Lately, I've been trying make my reading a little lighter, not in content but in weight. I have gathered some great stories that only require one good book: the Bible.

1. Bad hair day Judges 16:4–31—Samson has a secret. He gains his superhuman strength from his hair. Delilah, an Old Testament Mata Hari whom Samson loves very much, bribed by the leaders of the Philistines, discovers the source of Samson's strength, and sells out the man who loves her. This story of betrayal and justice tell of the unusual source of Samson's strength.

2. Wise ruling. 1 Kings 3:16–28—Read what happens when two women claim to be the mother of the same baby. Solomon, to whom this case is brought as Judge of Israel, knows that real love means sacrifice.

3. Curious cure. 2 Kings 5:1–27—Naaman, an Aramean general, goes to Israel to seek a cure on the advice of his servant girl, a Jewish girl who was captured in a raid against Israel. The king of Israel allows his journey but is worried that he is being set up to fail, thus giving the Syrians a pretext for war. In Luke's Gospel (Luke 4:27), Jesus uses this story to explain that salvation is meant for all. See if you can see the connection to our Sacrament of Baptism.

4. The great escape. Acts 12:1–17—King Herod thinks he can squash Christians by having them imprisoned and murdered. He has St. James, the brother of John, killed by a sword, but see what happens when he arrests St. Peter.

5. Shipwrecked. Acts 27–28—This is the story of Paul's journey to Rome as a prisoner. The story involves shipwreck, intrigue, and salvation. It will also make you feel better if you have any travel problems on your way to vacation!

CHAPTER 19

Avoid Getting Spiritually Dehydrated

It is easy to get dehydrated. We run around all day, and if we don't carry a water bottle, before we know it, we are bone-dry. Our spiritual life is the same. Pope Benedict XVI explains, "[I]n every person there is an inherent need for God and for salvation that only God can satisfy. It is a thirst for the infinite which only the water that Jesus offers, the living water of the Spirit, can quench."

The church in her wisdom has known this for a long time and has developed practices that help us remember to keep ourselves spiritually refreshed throughout the day. Remember, the Eucharist and quiet prayer are the ideal ways to quench a dry heart. However, the following five practices are well-tested ways of keeping us from getting spiritually dehydrated each day:

1. The examination of conscience. Although this is actually the last thing we should do each day, I place it first because it is so important and it lays the groundwork for a great next day. This is the method recommended by St. Ignatius of Loyola, and I think it works very well. First, say thanks to God for your day. Second, ask for the grace to know your sins and to move away from them. Third, play the movie of your day and recall all the great moments and the times you failed to love well. Fourth, tell God you're sorry. Fifth, make "The Plan" for tomorrow to love better. Be specific! Do not just say "I will be better tomorrow," but say "I will be better tomorrow in this specific area, to this person," etc. . . .

2. The morning offering. When you get up, before you brush your teeth, stop and thank God for the day and offer all that happens to him for his glory and your salvation. Recall "The Plan" from the night before. If you're not a morning person, put a Post-it on your mirror with *M.O.* written on it. If you're really not a morning person, put another Post-it with *M.O. = Morning Offering* on it.

3. The commute. When I listen to the traffic report in the morning, I not only think of all those people stuck on the highways; I also think of all the prayer potential each morning. The drive/ride/jog is a perfect time to say some extra prayers. Freestyle your own prayers, say your favorites, or maybe pray the Rosary. The good thing about a rosary is that it also keeps your finger busy when someone cuts you off.

4. Grace. "Bless us, O Lord, and these thy gifts which we have received from thy bounty through Christ our Lord. Amen." Now how hard was that? Pray before each meal and remember to cross yourself. Crossing yourself in public should not just be for professional athletes, and you may inspire a friend to know Jesus also.

5. The examination of conscience. It's so good it made the top-five list twice!

CHAPTER 20

Spiritual Exercises

I miss elementary school. Each day was a complete package. There was classwork, and then a bell rang and everyone got to go outside and play. Enjoying art and music were periods built into the week. If you went to a Catholic school, you had religion. You never had to schedule time to get exercise or read a book; it was all part of the day.

Praying for my archbishop to require all priests to go out at 10 a.m. to play in the yard is probably fruitless, so instead I must rely on my self-motivation, aided in large part by God's grace.

Growing in faith is not much different than trying to motivate myself for exercise. It's hard to make the time, but once I exercise and pray, I feel much better. I am better. The great news is that they don't have to be separate. A year of faith should turn into a long healthy life of faith. Time to multitask your way to health and heaven. Here are my five spiritual exercises:

1. Prayer walk/run. Pull out the earbuds and grab the beads. If you don't know it, learn to pray the Chaplet of Divine Mercy. It is very easy but very powerful. In the prayer we pray "for the whole world." As you make your way around the neighborhood or park, include every person you see whether you know them or not.

2. Strengthen the core. Much is said about building your core muscles, the muscles below the layers of fat on your belly. Situps help, but kneeling is also a great exercise. Now try kneeling in adoration of the Blessed Sacrament. Keep your back straight and your bum off the pew. Doing this before Jesus in the Eucharist strengthens the very core of our being in many ways.

3. Deep knee bends. The Stations of the Cross is not just for Lent. After you have prayed, "We adore you, O Christ, and we praise you," genuflect. Again, concentrate on posture so you don't pull anything. As you continue, "because by your Holy Cross you have redeemed the world," try not to grab the pew. Let the muscle burn be a mortification that joins you to Jesus' passion.

4. Wait training. Every day we find ourselves waiting. Maybe we are waiting in a doctor's office or for a friend to call. Almost everyone waits at a traffic light. These moments are perfect opportunities for wait training. Call to mind all the people you promised to pray for and start making good on your word. Make it a litany. Say their names and follow it with, "Have mercy on them." Try squeezing a tennis ball with each prayer to improve your grip strength for the sign of peace.

5. Power lifting. Lugging a box at the food pantry, mowing the elderly neighbor's lawn, and walking up the steps to deliver Holy Communion to the homebound are all amazing workouts. Pope Francis says, "True power, even in the Church, comes from serving others." Lift your power through service to others.

CHAPTER 21

New Year's Resolutions

I have heard a lot of people bad-mouthing resolutions over the years. Many people feel resolutions are ineffective. I get it. Although resolutions are usually New Year's dissolutions for me, I still want to try to become a better person. If change is the one thing we can count on, moving forward is the best option. Truth be told, if you think you are staying the same, odds are that you probably are moving backward. The book of Revelation expresses this in not-so-cheery language, "So, because you are lukewarm, neither hot nor cold, I will spit you out of my mouth" (3:16). I never liked spitting, so I am definitely setting a plan.

A few years back my parish set a plan by looking at five (go figure) areas of our parish life: community, worship, education, service, and administration. These areas are called "Indicators of Vitality." Simply put, we discerned that we could build up our community by strengthening our community. We began developing intergenerational events. For instance, older folks could ride with young adults to our picnics and special services. We got all different ages and interests involved on committees and volunteer opportunities. People got to know each other better, and we became a stronger family. The plan worked and continues to do so. We have doubled in size in the last six years.

If it is good enough for my people, it's good enough for me. With this in mind, let's do a self-study so that each of us can make a New Year's plan with our five ways to make solid resolutions:

1. Community. Remember in high school when they voted for Most Likely to Succeed, Best Dressed, etc.? If your family and neighbors were going to nominate you for a category, what would it be? Most Likely to Empty the Dishwasher? Biggest Complainer? Best Volunteer? Set a goal to be the best at something positive this year like noticing the good in others and spreading that news to others.

2. Worship. How much time of the week is spent on prayer? How much time is spent on TV? Maybe you pray a lot, but your mind wanders. It is very easy to get distracted at Mass. So many people doing such distracting things, coughing and wearing crazy outfits. If distraction is your prayer pothole, set a goal to work on it. How? When things enter your mind, turn them into a prayer. If Gladys is whispering during the homily, instead of blasting her, bless her with a prayer. "Dear God, please bless Gladys and all her loved ones." She may not shut up, but you will be holier.

3. Education. If I had one successful resolution this past year, it was to read more. Realizing that I had become substantially dumber than before, I turned off the tube and started working my way through my nightstand pile of books. Try reading more. If you already read, maybe it's time to test your mind in other ways, such as doing a puzzle with your coffee or trying your hand at a new hobby or physical activity. Muscles, including the brain, need exercise.

4. Service. In the letter of James we hear, "faith of itself, if it does not have works, is dead" (2:17). We can't just talk the talk; we need to walk the walk. Service is the hardest goal to set because it actually requires an investment of time, which is often harder to give than money. However, the payoff is greater. If you don't do anything or very little, this should be the prime goal. Usually, the parish bulletin is filled with opportunities. If not, call your priest and ask what needs getting done.

5. Administration/stewardship. Elvis Presley's motto was, "Taking care of business." I always liked Elvis, and I like this idea of focusing on what's important and getting things done. It could mean focusing on the work you do or getting exercise or cleaning out that crazy closet. As a family, we may need to reach out to an elderly relative. As a church, we need to evaluate our giving to the parish or our local community. As you work on stewardship, go ahead and give your hips a swing and say in your best Elvis impersonation, "Thank you. Thank you very much!"

CHAPTER 22

New Year's Restitutions

People often talk about "Catholic guilt." This bugs me. First, guilt isn't a bad thing. It keeps us from repeating wrong behavior. People without guilt are called sociopaths. Second, Catholicism has the Sacrament of Reconciliation meant to move people beyond guilt to love. Instead, people should talk about "Catholic forgiveness." This year, let's resolve to make a shift in our thinking.

While others may be dusting off their treadmills and joining gyms to fulfill their new (and probably recycled) New Year's resolutions, I suggest this year we all adopt instead some New Year's restitutions. Heaven is a grudge-free, junk-free state of being where baggage is not allowed. Jesus has won the victory, but it is up to us to live it freely. If we feel bad about something, it probably means that we should deal with it now. The time in this life is meant to get ready for the next.

When God forgives us in the Sacrament of Reconciliation, he cleanses us from our sins. In this gift he gives us the graces to help us love him and one another better. He also gives us the blessing and the courage to make things right. For example, if I stole ten dollars from you and went with sorrow and confessed it, God forgives me. However, that forgiveness does not automatically put money in your wallet. Our sin is like a nail in a wall. Reconciliation pulls the nail out, but there is still a hole left. Filling the hole is what we call restitution. When possible, we should make amends to those whom we have injured but if that is not possible, we should make restitution in some other way. The priest gives us a penance to do just this. This year let's go one step further:

1. Go to Mass during the week. If we have missed Sunday Mass or been late without a good reason or even if we did not pay attention, we should try to meet him at another time in the week. Jesus is truly present in the Mass so we should be truly present to him. A little inconvenience helps us notice reality.

2. Call or write that aunt, grandparent, dad, or old friend, whom you have been avoiding. The guilty feeling that pops into your head from time to time is an experience of unfulfilled love. You will not regret having loved even when it is hard.

3. For all the times you mentioned or noticed the negative, spread some good gossip. It is just as easy to say, "Aren't they wonderful?" as it is to say, "Can you believe what they said/did/wore . . . ?" Don't worry if it sounds fake at first; it is better than sounding mean.

4. Give to the poor. If you have ever taken a few things from work, taken some time away from a boss by not doing your job, sampled items that were not a sample at the grocery store, or did not return the change when you received too much, that's all stealing. Give that same amount of money or time to the poor.

5. Make small sacrifices. As I stand on my bathroom scale weeping from an overly celebrated Thanksgiving, Christmas, Hanukkah, or anything else I could celebrate, I realize that I do go overboard at times. For those times, offering up some small mortification helps us refocus. Go meatless on Fridays or empty the dishwasher even if it is not your job. Skip a meal or get up a bit early to read some Scripture. A little Lent out of season helps me remember how great and personal Jesus' love is for me.

Next time someone uses the phrase *Catholic guilt*, you may want to say, "You must mean *Catholic forgiveness*." If you've got it, don't be afraid to share it.

CHAPTER 23

Happy Birthday Gifts

Every year it rolls around. As a boy I would stare at the calendar of my birthday month and marvel at how time seemed to crawl along. Now I feel like it comes at me like a train barreling down the tracks. While I don't quite dread it, my birthday has lost some of its flare. It's time to rebrand birthdays. They should be moments to take stock and step forward in life, to transform birthdays into milestones of self-improvement. Celebrate each year as one of these years:

1. Year of the present. Sometimes it seems that we spend our lives waiting for the next thing and not living today. Waiting for graduation, the next raise, or retirement can take us away from living in the present more fully. Goals are good, but not if you're spending your time in yesterday or tomorrow and not enjoying today. Jesus is here today, so find him.

2. Year of charity. Cardinal Francis Van Thuan, the archbishop of Saigon, was imprisoned for thirteen years by the communist government in Vietnam from 1975–1988. Nine of those years were spent in solitary confinement. Although he was treated harshly, he decided that his uniform each day would be charity. He met his guards each day with a smile and kind words. Their cold hearts melted. I think of Cardinal Francis often when I see the world's impatience or coldness. Put on the uniform of charity this year.

3. Year of the family. Before you know it, the kids will be grown and gone. You won't be able to call your baby without having to talk to a daughter- or son-in-law. When that happens, you will not be thinking about the meetings you wish to attend or wishing that you had put them in another soccer league. When your kids or grandkids are grown, will they only remember the crazy number of activities that dominated their lives, or will they remember hanging out with you?

4. Year of the poor. Pope Francis talks a lot about our responsibility to the poor. He told some students in 2013, "Poverty in the world is a scandal. In a world where there is so much wealth, so many resources to feed everyone, it is unfathomable that there are so many hungry children, that there are so many children without an education, so many poor persons." As one who lives with so much, I am shaken from my slumber by Pope Francis and reminded that I need to take poverty seriously.

5. Year of joy. So often we look for things that make us happy, but they don't last that long. Eat a bag of cookies, and it won't be long before you're hungry again. Go to Mass during the week, start reading one of the Gospels, hang out with the kids, and you won't be hungry again. That's joy! At his midnight Mass on December 24, 2013, Pope Francis concluded his homily with these words, "On this night let us share the joy of the Gospel: God loves us, he so loves us that he gave us his Son to be our brother, to be light in our darkness." A year of joy means putting Jesus in the middle and keeping him there. If you do that, you and your family will know true joy, and who knows, you may even lose a little weight!

CHAPTER 24

St. Valentine's Day—Ways to Be Romantic Every Day

I never really understood the draw of St. Valentine's Day. Perhaps it is good that I am a celibate priest, because I don't see the charm in society dictating that you have to be romantic on a certain day. With a cultural gun to their temples, couples are told that the way to really love someone is to submit to this norm.

It seems to me that it would be much more romantic to give flowers or chocolates on a random Tuesday with a love note. Being forced to say, "I love you," is a lot like the apologies my parents used to force from us when my siblings and I were in a tussle. A gritted, "I am sorry," through clenched teeth hardly indicates true contrition.

I may go down in the annals of history as a Grinch that wrote off Valentine's Day. As my dog and I lug a sleigh full of hearts and bows up to our mountain cave, I will do so convinced that true romance should happen every day. I offer you five ways to be romantic on every day that isn't Valentine's Day:

1. Use pen and paper. A pen and paper are two of the most romantic tools in love's arsenal. Which do you think is more pleasing: a store-bought card or words written from your heart? If you're not sure what to say, go to the card shop, take a cell-phone photo of a mushy card, and copy it out in your own handwriting. Change a few words, and add your beloved's name. You are sure to melt a heart.

2. Do the dishes. While a romantic dinner is always a great gift, doing the dishes really says, "I love you enough to doing something I dislike." For courting couples, the way to the altar should be lined with dish soap bubbles.

3. Let your gift say, "I love you." Presents are a fabulous way to say, "I love you," but make sure that your beloved hears "I love you" with gifts. We may scrimp and save to buy a trinket or some jewelry, and what your love really wanted from you was to take out the trash. But, be careful, if your sweetie does like gifts and you give the gift of emptying the bin, you may be wearing its contents. Give your sweetheart what they want, not what you like.

4. Send a bouquet. I think flowers are always a winner, but don't just show up with a bunch of roses and think that you're done. Include a spiritual bouquet. For each rose, promise to say your beloved's favorite prayer.

5. Say it with chocolate and *vino*. Chocolate and good wine are both proof of God's existence. If your significant other doesn't like either, you may want to look for another mate. (If your love is just on a diet, simply drop the wine and chocolates by the rectory, and your pastor will make sure they go to good use.)

CHAPTER 25

Things to Get for Lent

People love to talk about "giving up" stuff for Lent. From candy to chardonnay, as Catholics it is our favorite Lenten conversation. Mortification, the ten-dollar word for disciplining our bodies and souls, is an important part of growing in holiness, but giving stuff up is not the only goal. Growing in the knowledge and love of Jesus Christ is the main point of Lent and beyond.

This year instead of just giving up, how about we get stuff for Lent. That's what I am doing this year. Come join me with five things to *get* for Lent:

1. Get busy. Often, we think of our spiritual lives like we think of a hobby. If I get time, I am going to work on prayer or my tennis game or my bagpipes or my French lessons. God is not going to ask us in French how our tennis serve is. Working on the spiritual life is the one thing that should be constantly improving. So it has to move up the priority list.

2. Get tough. With our priority list rearranged, when we acknowledge that prayer is not like golf but more like water and air, we need to figure out when we are going to actually pray. Get tough with yourself. Taking time out of the day is going to leave us strengthened to live our day more fully. Surprisingly, the more time you give to God, the more you get things done. Try it.

3. Get excited. Each day when I go to pray, I stop and just experience the silence. It's like slipping into a hot tub. With so much noise in the world and in my heart, the gift of quiet is luxurious. Get excited to dwell in that peace each day.

4. Get full. The Second Vatican Council referred to the Eucharist as "the source and summit" of the Christian life. Jesus is truly present in the Eucharist, body, blood, soul, and divinity. Increasing our experience of the Eucharist through daily Mass and times of prayer before the tabernacle or at adoration will deliver the mother lode of grace for your life.

5. Get happy. At the end of the day, joy is what we really desire and what God desires for us. Jesus knew this when he told us, "If you keep my commandments, you will remain in my love, just as I have kept my Father's commandments and remain in his love. I have told you this so that my joy may be in you and your joy may be complete" (John 15:10–11). Prayer is not just about my peace but building the Kingdom of God. During Lent, connect with God and then help others do the same by inviting them back home to the church.

CHAPTER 26

Make Every Week a Holy Week

Holy Week is a power punch of grace. Starting with Palm Sunday and moving through Holy Thursday and Good Friday to Easter, each step is filled with signs and symbols that explain how deeply we are loved by God. Holy Week helps us experience our dignity as God's sons and daughters and the destiny we are called to as saints in heaven.

It's easy for Holy Week to be a week that is special but then passes into memory. However, it actually is a gift that is given in one week and takes a whole year to unwrap. To help with this, here are five ways to make every week a Holy Week:

1. "Hosanna to the Son of David." We hear this line from Matthew 21:9 on Palm Sunday. The crowds shout this when Jesus enters Jerusalem. A few days later they turn and we hear, "Crucify him!" Their fickle nature should ring a bell. How is it that we can sometimes be so kind and other times be petty, jealous, gossipy, and grudge holding? It's called Original Sin. We are made for love, yet often we choose otherwise. Knowing the problem is the main part of the solution. Pick the most persistent struggle, the thing you say sorry for the most, and decide to leave it at the foot of the Cross. Then start working to build up the opposite blessing. For example, if you are critical from time to time in your head, start working on noticing and commenting on the good in others.

2. Washing of the feet. On Holy Thursday, Jesus gives his church the priesthood, and he explains to his apostles how they are to lead through service. This model should be the basis for all we do. It's not just priests who are ordained to serve, but all the baptized are to do so as well. In essence we have been baptized to be inconvenienced. Go the extra mile: volunteer to help a homebound friend walk her dog, stop and talk to the neighbor even when you're feeling busy. Each inconvenience is a way for us to wash Jesus' feet this time.

3. Take this, all of you. With these words, Jesus gives us the Eucharist. On the Cross, Jesus offers himself as a sacrifice for our sins. He gives us the Mass so that we can participate in his victory without having to die on the Cross ourselves. Our gifts placed on the altar become his gift to all humanity. He is truly present in body, blood, soul, and divinity. Try extra hard to be conscious of the great mystery and the gift we receive. Get to church a little early, be conscious of the fast, and stay a few minutes later to say thanks.

4. Easter fire. The Great Easter Vigil, the first Mass of Easter, begins with the lighting of the paschal fire. From it we light the paschal candle. The fire reminds us of God's generous initiative in creating us and his overwhelming mercy of recreating us after we have sinned. Jesus is the light of the world. This year we should try to shine his light to the world. Light and snarky comments don't go together. Greet people with a smile and avoid commenting to others when they don't treat you the same way.

5. Holy water. At the Easter Masses we renounce sin, renew our baptismal promises, and are sprinkled with holy water.

We recall our Baptism so that we can remember that it is this moment where we became part of Christ for all eternity. Each time we enter church, we bless ourselves with holy water again. As we make the Sign of the Cross, we usually are looking for our seats while simultaneously checking out who is also at Mass. Try to be conscious in that moment that you are renewing your Baptism. Quickly renounce Satan and sin, and with a smile say, "I believe," because every week should be a Holy Week.

CHAPTER 27

Getting the Most Out of Easter

We have been fasting, praying and almsgiving for six long weeks with one goal in mind: Easter. In case you forgot, the point of Lent is to prepare to celebrate the Lord's Resurrection most fully. Holy Thursday, Good Friday, and the Easter Vigil constitute the three most holy days of the year. Together, the experience is called the Triduum, or three days. Actually, the Mass of the Lord's Supper (Holy Thursday), the Celebration of the Lord's Passion (Good Friday), and the Easter Vigil comprise one complete experience.

Here are five ways to get the most out of Easter:

1. Book yourself. Take out your calendar and commit yourself to attending Holy Thursday and Good Friday services. Since Easter is already an obligation, you will be going. If you have never attended the Great Easter Vigil, it is well named because it is great.

2. Holy Thursday. Since you will now be attending the Mass of the Lord's Supper, stick around and pray for just a few minutes after Mass and say a prayer for the priests in your life. On Holy Thursday our Lord gave us the Eucharist, and in order to give us the Eucharist, he instituted the priesthood. It's the birthday of all priests.

3. Good Friday. Good Friday is supposed to feel a bit empty and sad. Try to imagine what Jesus was feeling this day. All his friends have run away, and only his Blessed Mother, St. John the Beloved, and a few women remain at the foot of the Cross. All the while, he is doing this for you and me, not in a generic way but truly thinking of you and me as he dies to make us whole. It's sad so don't be afraid of it.

4. Holy Saturday. Try to stop by your parish in the morning and feel how empty it is without the Blessed Sacrament in the tabernacle. The world is hauntingly still as

Jesus has entered into death so that we may have eternal life. Be quiet for a little bit and pray never to forget how empty we would be if Christ had never risen from the dead.

5. Easter party! You have sat with Jesus in the upper room as he has given us the memorial of his sacrifice and the priesthood to perpetuate in the Mass. You have walked to Calvary and sat at the foot of the Cross and watched him die for our sins. It is now Easter, and the tomb is empty. That means that death is not the end. Life and love, forgiveness and justice will always win. You will see again those who have died. The end of the story is really the beginning—eternal life—so start celebrating!

CHAPTER 28

A First Advent

I have never had a baby. Since I am a priest, I am sure you are grateful for that news! But I do have twenty-two nieces and nephews and seven great ones. (They're all great, but these ones are the next generation.) Although I have no firsthand knowledge of gestation, I have seen enough pregnant moms to know that the last month is not easy. While Advent is a time of preparation, think back to the first Advent and picture Mary. She was not decorating a tree or making Christmas gift lists. She was on her way to Bethlehem because Caesar had called for a census, so Joseph and Mary had to return to his home city. That could not have been pleasant.

Perhaps we can get more out of Advent this year if we spend a little time meditating on the first Advent and spending quality time with our Blessed Mother. Here are five ways to get you started:

1. Be thankful for sleep. One thing I have heard from many expecting mothers is that it's hard to get sleep when you are in your last month of pregnancy. It's just hard to get comfortable, and there's always some heartburn. Peaceful rest is a great gift and when it doesn't come, it is stressful. Mary may have struggled to sleep too. If you find yourself unable to get those *Zzzzzs,* remember the words of Mary as she greeted her cousin Elizabeth, "My soul proclaims the greatness of the Lord, my spirit rejoices in God my savior" (Luke 1:46–47). Then call to mind the blessings of your life. If you find your mind wandering, repeat Mary's words and continue. You may not fall asleep, but why not do some praying since you have that time anyway.

2. Ouch, that hurts! Riding on a donkey is not comfortable, especially, I would imagine, for a long trip. How about riding a donkey on a long trip when you're nine months pregnant! The trip to Christmas is not always easy. Try to remember that small moments of inconvenience can actually be opportunities for great grace. In a long line at the DMV, say a Litany of the Saints. Just randomly call to mind your favorite saints, and then say, "Pray for us (or her or me)." Waiting for a doctor's appointment, repeat the Angelus to yourself (and to Mary). You can turn dead time into eternal lifetime.

3. Get a *fiat!* Here's an old joke. "How did the Holy Family get to Bethlehem? By Mary's *fiat!*" Explanation: Mary's yes to God was, "Thy will be done," which in Latin is, *Fiat voluntas tua.* Oh, and a Fiat is a type of car. Get it? I didn't say it was funny, I said it was old. But the point is that we need to rev up our *fiats*, our yeses to God. This Advent don't forget the poor. Remember to put money in the poor box in your parish or donate to Catholic Charities or a local food bank. Say *yes* to God by helping the poor.

4. Get to a house of bread. Did you know that Bethlehem means "house of bread"? How great that Christ be born in the house of bread when he truly gives himself to us in the form of bread in the Eucharist. The church is the new Bethlehem, the house of bread, where Christ is born again anew at every Mass. So, as Mary and Joseph head to Bethlehem, accompany them by going to your local "house of bread" for an extra Mass or two during the week this Advent.

5. Keep Jesus out of the NICU! I had two great-nephews born sixteen weeks premature. The doctors and nurses who work in the Neonatal Intensive Care Units (NICU) are amazing people, so strong yet so gentle. Thank God, the boys are fine, but the road was very stressful for everyone, especially their mom and dad. While the malls and radio stations want Jesus to be born sometime between Halloween and Thanksgiving, we Catholics prefer full term. Advent is time a preparation in advance of the celebration. Follow the readings of each day from Mass, pray a bit more, and even considering giving something up so that when we party at Christmas, we can be aware of how blessed we are to have Jesus Christ as our Savior. Help Jesus to go full-term by actually experiencing a complete and holy Advent.

Christmas Gifts for Your Priest

Two ingredients that have become central to the celebration of Jesus' birth are fat and sugar. I bemoan this not because I do not like fat and sugar, but because I really like foods that have lots of fat and sugar. Celebrating a feast historically included such things because the feast had been preceded by a period of fasting. However, Christmas now is preceded by Thanksgiving and a bunch of Christmas parties.

With a priest shortage, I would like to recommend some things to get for your priest that do not involve sugar or fat (These words were difficult to write, but I managed through the grace of the Holy Spirit!):

1. Your neighbor. Bring your neighbor to Mass and introduce him or her to the priest. Growing numbers and a new soul tops even a cream pie.

2. A spiritual bouquet. A note with a promise to say some prayers for your priests is a wonderful Christmas gift. Quite frankly, looking at our world, it is clear that some serious spiritual battles are going on. Your prayers are the invisible powerhouse that allows the priest to face the most difficult situations with joy. If your pastor is a bit grumpy, maybe it is because you don't pray for him enough.

3. Live your Baptism. I pray each day for my parish not only that they will come to Mass and receive Jesus in the Eucharist, but also that they will bring him to the world. As Jesus is the great high priest, this gift is probably more for him than just for your local pastor. Being a great mom/dad/son/daughter/friend/employee/boss and being truly a person of faith is a challenge. But heroes and saints are people who face challenges. So, stand up and tell the world that you're proud to be a follower of Jesus. Let people see how you love his church. Say grace before meals, go to Mass while on vacation. Make a list of people who need your prayers and pray it with your kids each night. Defend the faith.

4. Encourage and pray for vocations. We just opened Blessed John Paul II Seminary in the Archdiocese of Washington because we have good numbers of men following the Lord to discern a call to the priesthood. The movement of the Holy Spirit is clear, but we need to pray that young men will be preserved from things that block them from hearing Christ's call. This is where you come in. Encouragement of a young man and prayers for those already in the seminary must be part of your daily regime. This is a great gift not only to the seminarians but to the whole archdiocese.

5. Food for the poor. Write a note to the priest: "I gave your cookies to the hungry." Once his blood pressure lowers, which it probably needs to anyway, he will be very grateful. We need your generosity more than we need your chocolate chips. (Once again, the Holy Spirit helped me pen that sentence.)

CHAPTER 30

Christmas Sound Bites

A sound bite is a short audio or video clip used often for news reports. They are quick but can encapsulate a powerful message. There was little initial coverage of one of the most important events in human history, the birth of the Savior of the world. However, some of the quotes that came out of that miraculous time are full of grace. As a Christmas present, I give you five Christmas sound bites:

1. "He will be great and will be called Son of the Most High" (Luke 1:32). These are the words that the angel Gabriel speaks to Mary. Her son is the Son of God. This means that God truly comes to save us. Jesus is no mere prophet, a wise teacher; he is God. That is how much we are loved. God does not send a representative; he sends his only begotten Son.

2. "She will bear a son and you are to name him Jesus, because he will save his people from their sins" (Matt. 1:21). This sound bite comes from the angel who appears to Joseph in a dream. When Joseph finds out that Mary is pregnant, he has second thoughts, but the angel explains not only the divine origin of Jesus but also his mission. He is coming because we are sinners, lost with no way to get home. This ministry continues through the ages in the sacraments of the church.

3. "Do not be afraid; for behold, I proclaim to you good news of great joy that will be for all the people" (Luke 2:10). We capture this sound bite while the angel is announcing the Messiah's birth to the shepherds. In Latin, the words of the angel proclaiming good news of great joy are *Evangelizo vobis gaudium magnum*. The word *evangelizo* means to bring good news. In recent years, evangelization has been misunderstood as forcing our beliefs in a judgmental way on others, but this is not the case. The angel does not force or coerce; the angel invites. Welcoming others to Mass, inviting them home, is part of our duty as followers of Jesus.

4. "And this will be a sign for you: you will find an infant wrapped in swaddling clothes and lying in a manger" (Luke 2:12). Again, the angel is speaking to the shepherds. What stands out is that the baby is not in a crib or in his mother's arms or on some hay. The baby is in the manger, which is the feeding place for the animals. The connection is obscure but powerful; Jesus will be the food of salvation. Already, God is preparing us to meet Jesus in the Mass in the Eucharist.

5. "Let us go, then, to Bethlehem to see this thing that has taken place, which the Lord has made known to us" (Luke 2:15). The shepherds are on their way to find the Christ when we capture this sound bite. The next time you receive Communion, say a special prayer of thanksgiving because that same Jesus in the arms of Mary is now truly held in your body, too.

CHAPTER 31

Christmas with St. Joseph

From time to time you hear about babies being born in a car on the way to the hospital. Suddenly, an expectant father becomes an obstetrician. While those moments must be very stressful, I imagine that the back seat of a modern-day car must seem like the Mayo Clinic compared to a stable in Bethlehem. I don't think that St. Joseph gets enough credit for making the Christmas story a happy one, so I offer you my five reflections for spending Christmas with St. Joseph:

1. Sore feet. I have never ridden a donkey before, but I imagine that there is not much room for anyone besides a pregnant woman. The trip to the delivery stable was not short. Google Maps puts it at over ninety miles of walking. Luke's Gospel does not indicate that Mary was in active labor during the trip, but nonetheless Joseph did all the walking. Remember that getting things ready for Christmas can be exhausting, but don't add to the stress of the delivery by being cranky. I guarantee you that Joseph didn't complain.

2. No reservations. We know for a fact that the Holy Family had no reservations, so Joseph had to do some quick thinking. Flexibility is the first ingredient to lowering holiday stress. This Christmas expect the unexpected, say a little prayer to St. Joseph, and go with the flow. When things turn upside down, you'll smile and not frown.

3. There's company coming. After Jesus was born, there were a lot of visitors. First the shepherds showed up, next the Magi, and all along a multitude of Heavenly Hosts were enjoying the view. A little alone time is a nice thing, but it may not happen this year. Enjoy any calm before the storm. Don't just lie on your bed and nap; spiritually rest. Say your favorite prayer slowly (mine is the Memorare), and ask the newborn Prince of Peace to let his peace stay with you when you are in the midst of a big crowd, especially if that crowd is related to you.

4. Away from home. Joseph and his young family were away from their friends when Jesus was born. Many people are alone on Christmas, and for some this is very challenging. If you're not one of those people, stop and think if you know someone who will be alone, and invite them over for a little Christmas cheer. I am of the opinion that someone outside the family at the Christmas table puts everyone else on their best behavior. If you will be alone this Christmas, remember that you're never alone. In prayer, spend some time with the Holy Family in their solitude. Holidays need not be lonely. You can actually make Christmas an intentional spiritual retreat, a planned time of prayer with the best company imaginable.

5. No delivery. I am not talking about the baby; I mean dinner. New moms need to eat and drink to regain their strength. The Gospels make no mention of a Domino's delivery camel showing up outside the stable. Joseph shopped, cooked, and cleaned. If that is your Christmas job assignment, be grateful because you're in such great company. If you normally don't help with these things, put down your eggnog, get your lazy self off the couch and say these simple words, "I will do the dishes." Think of it as doing Jesus' dishes.

CHAPTER 32

Perspectives on Mass Etiquette

1. Wear clothes. 2. Don't text during Mass. 3. Yes, drinking coffee breaks the fast before receiving Communion, so don't carry Starbucks into church. 4. Smile at people, because we believe in Jesus. These are just a few of the gripes that an average priest might add to the etiquette list. However, my perspective is not your perspective. Although I cannot read minds, I have heard the thoughts of many parishioners on what they would like the world to know from their point of view.

Here are five different perspectives on Mass etiquette:

1. Mom with kids: "I am trying my best. Most of my friends don't even bother. Please remember that the sound of antsy kids is the sound of a family at prayer."

2. Old man without kids: "My hearing aid cannot differentiate between your baby and the priest. If your kid is having a tantrum, a mini-tantrum, or just discovered his echo in the church, please take your bundle of joy to a place where he or she can quiet down. But hurry back because that child is the future of the church."

3. Usher: "I am not getting paid. I am not the janitor or the bellhop. Pick up your tissues, your water bottles, the *Catholic Standard* you read during the homily, and your bits of Cheerios. I want to get home after Mass also."

4. Priest: "I love saying hello to everyone at the end of Mass. However, if you have something to say that takes longer than, 'Father, that was the best homily I have ever heard,' please wait for the crowd to pass or call for an appointment."

5. God: "I am so glad you're here. I love you."

CHAPTER 33

When the Big Game Is On

Whether it's the Stanley Cup, the World Series, March Madness, the Super Bowl, or the final game of the Pee Wee League, there are a few things you need to remember. Yes, there is food to be eaten and commercials to be watched. Office pools should be organized and faces should be painted, but there are also five things to keep in mind and heart when the big game is on:

1. Mass. The Super Bowl or World Series does not dispense you from the obligation to attend Holy Mass.

2. Stay focused. If your team wins, remember how St. Thomas Aquinas said the sin of pride is the root of all sins. So please don't push your big foam finger in the face of fans from the other team. If your team loses, remember that humility is a gift, so receive it gratefully.

3. Confirmation. At our Confirmation we receive the seven Gifts of the Holy Spirit. These are wisdom, understanding, right judgment, courage, knowledge, reverence, wonder, and awe in God's presence. Notice that "being an expert on all things sports" is not on the list. Again, stay humble.

4. Use your time wisely. If your favorite season is soon to end, you may have four more hours in your week. If you're married, spend some extra time with your spouse. If you're not married, take a class or volunteer. If you're a priest, go get some exercise because people need you to live a long time.

5. Last rites. If your team loses, remember you are not dead. The next sport season begins tomorrow.

CHAPTER 34

Learn to Love Confession

Sometimes we think of sin as the bad side of ourselves. That is wrong. Sin is not who we are. It is who we are *not*.

Think of yourself as a pipe. A pipe brings water from one place to another. Gunk, goop, and gross stuff are not the pipe. They are the things that get stuck in the pipe and constrict the water. The water is God's love. You are the instrument he wishes to use to get his love out to your family and the world. The goop and gunk are your sins. Some sins are big clogs that shut down the flow completely, and some are smaller sins that hamper grace in your life. Either way, it's not good.

The Sacrament of Reconciliation is like Drano. It gets rid of all that is not you, so that God can use you fully each day to give his love and your gifts and talents to the world. Here are five things I love about going to confession:

1. The seal. The priest cannot ever tell what was said in the Sacrament of Reconciliation. Period. You can say whatever you need to say, no matter how bad.

2. Priests have bad memories. I am not sure whether it is forgetfulness or the fact that priests are more concerned with forgiving than remembering your sins, but it's good either way.

3. Not just for Lent and Advent. I try to go every week or two. I like the water flow to be strong. The stakes are high. If people meet a Christian with restricted water flow, to use the pipe metaphor again, they might not ever meet Christ.

4. Two for the price of one. When I receive absolution, not only does Jesus take away my sins, but also he gives me special sacramental graces to live up to the potential that both God and I know that I can achieve.

5. It's free.

CHAPTER 35

Essential School Supplies

For parents, it happens every year—the pilgrimage to get your kids' new shoes, binders, and lunch boxes. While you're getting the kids ready for school, may I also suggest five other essential school necessities:

1. Holy medal. Wearing a holy medal is a part of Catholic culture. Whether it's the miraculous medal of our Lady, a patron saint, or a crucifix, a holy medal is a physical reminder that God is always with us. Tell the kids that you want to give them a special gift for school. Use this as an opportunity to talk about patron saints, our Blessed Mother, or our Lord's sacrifice on the Cross. While you're at it, get one for yourself.

2. Grace. Type or write the prayer before meals. You know, the standard, "Bless us, O Lord . . ." and tape it inside their lunch boxes. Encourage them to pray the prayer before diving into lunch. Teaching them to make the Sign of the Cross will give them courage to stand up for Jesus and for themselves later in life when they are faced with greater challenges.

3. Time. When I was little, we had one activity or sport a season. Now it seems like my nieces and nephews have to be in three soccer leagues all at once. Give them the gift of playing outside that is just playing. Give them the gift of free time to just be a kid.

4. More time. Life is busy for parents. I always tell younger clergy who feel that they are running around all day, "You're not busy. Look at the parents in your parish. *That's* busy." Although carpools are a great time-saver, I am not sure it's the time that you want to save. Car time is sacred time. It's you and your kids. Turn off the radio, forbid earphones, and find out what is really going on in their lives.

5. Potential. How can potential be a school supply? Education is all about reaching our potential. Reaching our potential means becoming the people God knows we can be and desires us to be. We reach our goals by periodically evaluating our performance, further developing the strategies that work, and abandoning things or behaviors that don't work. It's why we have report cards. But it is also the strategy of the moral life. Evaluating ourselves, developing virtue, and avoiding vice is part of how Jesus saves us. He gave us an amazing tool to make this easy and the grace to help us succeed. It's called confession. Before the school year begins, talk to your children about their gifts, their potential, and get the whole family to confession. Go again together each month. God's grace in helping your kid become the best person he or she can be is the most essential school supply of all.

CHAPTER 36

Musts for the Newly Engaged

I estimate that I have presided at more than 350 weddings. I think I have seen it all, from brides in cowboy boots and Western wear to Civil War recreationists who came down the aisle looking like Rhett Butler and Scarlett O'Hara. I like doing weddings because you walk with couples on their most important journey, their vocation to God and to each other. Over time, I have come to see the elements that make for a great wedding, and so I share with you my five musts for the newly engaged:

1. Call the priest first. This is often the biggest mistake that couples make. They book a reception venue and then try to find a church to match. While some may attribute this to mixed-up priorities, I prefer to think that it's just inexperience. It's harder to find a priest than a reception hall.

2. You're planning a marriage, not a wedding. So much effort goes into napkin colors and flower displays, and the most important part is marriage preparation. Have an all-in attitude when you take the classes and meet with the priest.

3. Make the honeymoon a honeymoon. Couples who live together before marriage have the highest divorce rate. I think this is because there is no big adjustment after the wedding, so there is not the interior realization of how big a step marriage is. Couples who have to negotiate over closet space the week after the honeymoon realize that the wedding was a huge step in life.

4. Don't shortchange God. Pray about the percentage of your budget for the wedding that you are going to donate to the church. It is wrong if you spend more on a dress that you wear once or the booze or limos than you return to God. Parishes don't invest profits; they pay the bills, help the poor, and run schools. Make that a part of your wedding.

5. Go to Mass. Authenticity is the key to a beautiful wedding. Couples who go to Mass regularly are at home on the day of the wedding. The ceremony has an empty feel when a couple's last time at Mass was at Easter. If you want to get married in the church, go to church. If the church is just a backdrop and not part of your life, I think Vegas might be a more honest option. Make Mass your best date of the week. Go to the Saturday vigil and have dinner afterward, or get up and finish Mass with brunch or quiet time in the park. We are Roman Catholic for a reason because we're so *roman*tic!

CHAPTER 37

Tips for a Great Wedding

St. John's Gospel tells us that Jesus attended a wedding in Cana in Galilee. (This is why marriage prep is sometimes called pre-Cana.) It was here that he performed his first miracle by changing water into wine. In case you're a bit rusty on the story, here's what John writes:

When the wine ran short, the mother of Jesus said to him, "They have no wine."

[And] Jesus said to her, "Woman, how does your concern affect me? My hour has not yet come." His mother said to the servers, "Do whatever he tells you." Now there were six stone water jars there for Jewish ceremonial washings, each holding twenty to thirty gallons. Jesus told them, "Fill the jars with water." So they filled them to the brim. Then he told them, "Draw some out now and take it to the headwaiter." So they took it. And when the headwaiter tasted the water that had become wine, without knowing where it came from (although the servers who had drawn the water knew), the headwaiter called the bridegroom and said to him, "Everyone serves good wine first, and then when people have drunk freely, an inferior one; but you have kept the good wine until now." Jesus did this as the beginning of his signs in Cana in Galilee and so revealed his glory, and his disciples began to believe in him. (John 2:3–11)

Here are my five tips for a great wedding:

1. Expect something to go wrong. Perfection only happens in heaven. If you expect a perfect day, week, or life, you're only going to be disappointed. If Jesus is invited, you can *always* work things out.

2. Invite Mary. Ever since that wedding, Mary has been interceding for couples who turn to her. Start now by praying a Hail Mary together when you say goodbye at night. Name the worries and wishes of your heart and ask her to bring them to her Son.

3. Fill the jars. Gifts are a part of weddings, but I suggest that the brides and grooms should not just be out for the take. Instead to try to be out for the give. Budget for a gift to the poor when you plan your wedding expenses. When planning the bachelor/ette party, in addition to a fun party, why not spend the day at the soup kitchen or food pantry? As part of marriage prep, fill someone else's jar.

4. 6 jars x 25 gallons = 150 gallons. At five bottles per gallon, that equals 750 bottles of wine. Wow! Regardless of exactly how much wine Jesus made, the point is that letting Jesus Christ into the empty jars of our hearts results in a superabundance of joy. No cakes or dresses or perfect reception site will do that, so don't lose perspective on what's important.

5. Save the best wine for last. Good things are worth waiting for, especially honeymoons. 'Nuff said.

CHAPTER 38

Myths of the Priesthood

I recently attended the ordination of five men to the priesthood. It was a wonderful celebration and a beautiful cause for reflection on the gift of Holy Orders. After nineteen years of being a priest, I realize that Catholics have no idea what we do all day or what our lives are like. So, here I debunk five myths of the priesthood:

1. Priests are lonely. Some are, but so are some married people. It's not the state of life that makes someone lonely; it is the decisions they make. Like anyone else, I have to keep a regular prayer life. Since who I am and what I do depends on a singular relationship with Christ, I'd better have that relationship. I also have to make sure that I get out and keep up with friends, but for most priests I know, it is alone time they need more than too much company.

2. Priest are holier than other people. This myth is based on a false precept that holiness is quantifiable. There is no holy-o-meter that tells me when I am holy enough or more holy than someone else. We are all called to holiness. It's not just for priests and those in religious life. Each person must find quiet time to spend with Jesus in prayer. It is not a luxury; it is a necessity, like water or air. This time of intimacy feeds our day, which is in reality a mission flowing from that prayer, a mission to be a mom, dad, aunt, uncle, businessperson, judge, doctor, priest, or whatever. We are all called to be holy.

3. Priests are just interested in religion. The priest who only talks, reads, or thinks about religion probably gives boring homilies. The priest who is keenly aware of the presence of God in church and also in life and all the wonderful things that are in it will truly move hearts.

4. Priests only work one day a week. Would that it were true! There is a profound need and hunger for Christ's love in this world. A wise priest friend told me when I was a seminarian, "Say 'Yes' until you have to say 'No.'" I try to follow that advice every day, and my golf game has suffered.

5. Priests wear black knee socks on the beach. Actually, sometimes they're white.

CHAPTER 39

Graduation Presents

Whether you're moving from kindergarten to first grade or you just finished your Ph.D., graduations are a time for celebration. My graduation present this year is not cash or a briefcase; it's five tips to keep in mind as you set forth on a new part of life's journey. These equally apply to six-, twenty-six-, or eighty-six-year-old grads:

1. It isn't easy. Change is exciting, but it is also hard. Whenever we move to a new adventure, we say goodbye to a familiar way of living. In a sense it is a little death, so it's OK to mourn the old life. Just remember that this hidden sadness can come out in grouchy ways. Just consider that the new adventure can be as fabulous as the old one, too.

2. Lose the training wheels. This new phase of life involves stretching yourself. Make room for the new by losing an old crutch or two. This could be sugar, smokes, T.V., or too much internet. When trying to shake up something in my life, it is essential I tell someone and give him or her permission to bug me about it. God gave us best friends not just to have fun with, but also to help us be better disciples.

3. Hit the road, Jack(y). Travel. Travel. Travel. I am not talking about going to the beach. I say, see the world. Save up your pennies, skip a latte or two, and before you know it you will have enough for a bus trip to New York or a trek in Burma. The important part of traveling the world is that you learn you're not the center of it.

4. Find a vocation, not just a job. Christ is calling you to something special, a way of life that builds up his kingdom. It may be married life, priesthood, religious life, or perhaps a consecrated single life. Being a teacher, lawyer, or a doctor is not a vocation; it's part of a vocation. The bottom line is that at the end of your life, God is not going to ask to see your résumé; he's going to ask who you brought with you.

5. Adulthood is actually great. I like being in my fifties better than my twenties. Don't get me wrong; I have enjoyed every stage of my life, even adolescence. But I feel like I am wiser, and wiser is better. Intelligence shows a great mind. Wisdom demonstrates a great soul, and there is no true wisdom without God. To that end, graduate, go to Mass every Sunday and pray every day. God makes you great.

CHAPTER 40

Every Year Is a Year of Faith

Some years ago, Pope Benedict XVI declared a Year of Faith from October 11, 2012, until November 24, 2013. From time to time, the church celebrates such a year, to grow in the knowledge and love of Jesus Christ around a particular theme. Just because the year has passed does not mean we can't keep it up.

Faith is a gift and, like hope and love, it is given to us in our Baptisms. Faith is also a decision. The more we share love, the more love grows in our lives. So, too, the more we share our faith, the greater our faith will be. With this in mind, I offer you five ways to make every year a year of faith:

1. Remember. Most of us don't remember our Baptism, but we should remind ourselves from time to time that we are baptized. If we call ourselves Catholics, we believe Jesus is the Son of God, sent to redeem the world. Otherwise, he was the biggest con man in history. The choice is simple. The answer makes all the difference in this world and the next.

2. Learn. When Jesus says, "I am the way, the truth, and the life" (John 14:6), he does not say that he's "*a* way" or "*a* truth" or "*a* life." We have to learn why his message is *the* message, the secret to happiness, and not just one gate among many to enter the Kingdom of God. Jesus, even to those who have never heard of him, is the only bridge between heaven and earth. So, it is time to learn more about him. Read one of the Gospels this year. Sacred Scripture is not just the story of what happened two thousand years ago; it is the living Word of God seeking to enlighten your heart and mind in a new way. Matthew, Mark, Luke, and John have something to show you. Start at the beginning and slowly read a bit more each day. Don't rush it.

3. Pray. Mother Teresa once said, "When we look at the Cross, we know how much Jesus loved us. When we look at the tabernacle, we know how much Jesus loves us now." In the Eucharist, Jesus is truly present body, blood, soul, and divinity. So, if you want to deepen your faith, expand your experience of the source and goal of that faith: Jesus. Try going to Mass one day during the week that isn't Sunday.

4. Serve. In his letter, St. James asks, "What good is it, my brothers, if someone says he has faith but does not have works?" Yikes, that means Mass alone does not cut it. Time to look in the bulletin and see what service opportunities there are. Make food for the poor, visit the homebound, or sign up for a holy hour? It's all good; just pick one and give it a try.

5. Share. If a movie star or famous athlete showed up on your doorstep wanting to meet you, wouldn't you tell someone about it? How about if God came to meet you? Well, he did and does. He is in the church, his Mystical Body. He is in the Eucharist at Mass, in our prayer with the Scripture, and in our neighbor who needs us. It would be a pity if someone did not get to meet him because I never said anything. It won't be a year of faith if you don't share the faith.

CHAPTER 41

Ways to Be a Genius

Sometimes I pick a topic or person I know very little about and try to learn something new—for example, Albert Einstein. I once read a book about the famous scientist and while I may not understand his theory of relativity well, I have learned a few other things that for me are equally important. Being a genius in science does not necessarily make you one in life. Einstein discovered the $E = mc^2$, but I am not sure he understood that *Dad = Time + Kid*. I am not trying to be unkind or judgmental because Einstein lived in a different time and emotional place than we do now, but he wasn't the best father. It is clear to me that we are all called to be geniuses in our own way, so I offer five ways to be a genius:

1. Nice Kids = Quality Time + Quantity Time. This is not easy in our busy world. With work and sports teams, homework and friends, getting enough time with your children is a real challenge. It breaks my heart to pull up to a stoplight and see a teenager sitting in the front passenger seat with headphones on or staring at a cell phone. An opportunity missed is gone forever. We need to maximize every opportunity. Maybe Junior does not need to do more than one activity/sport a season? Maybe the kids need less screen time. Set parameters and spend quality time with your kids just talking or going for a walk. And if you're reading this, and you realize that you weren't such a fantastic parent, you can always be an incredible grandparent.

2. Marriage = You + God's Love. God gives husbands and wives to each other to allow them to show his love in a unique and personal way. Only a spouse can love the other in this special way. From that love flows everything in the couple's life: children, joy, and, especially eternal life. Married couples must cultivate the sacredness of their vows each day.

3. Gospel = You + Inconvenience + Neighbor. When I say neighbors, I mean not just the people that live next door. Neighbors includes everybody that is not family.

Going out of our way to be kind is the reason we were baptized. St. Paul writes, "Let love be sincere; hate what is evil, hold on to what is good; love one another with mutual affection; anticipate one another in showing honor" (Rom. 12:9–10). This means we have to think of serving others, both those we like and those we don't like, as the means of serving Jesus.

4. Heaven = You + Poor. This is equation is simple but also very hard. As Pope Francis reminds us, "Poverty is the flesh of the poor Jesus, in that child who is hungry, in the one who is sick, in those unjust social structures."

5. God's Love = Infinite. This is the most important equation of all. I learned this from my best theology professor. She didn't have a doctorate; in fact she could neither read nor write, but Maria was a genius in God. She lived in a shack with a dirt floor in a small town in Nicaragua where I spent a summer during seminary. When I went to bring her Holy Communion, she exclaimed, "Today my home is a castle because the King of kings has come to visit me!" I learned that day, as I have each day of my priesthood, that I have a lot to learn about the mercy and love of Jesus Christ. Each day the Lord invites us on a journey deeper into that mystery. All we have to say is, "Yes, Lord, I believe. Make me a genius in you."

CHAPTER 42

Exercise Your Rights . . . to Rest!

We have a lot of holidays in our country. All of us need a day of rest. God already gave us one each week: Sunday. The problem is that we have transformed Sunday into Run-day, an errand-filled, catch-up-on-work period of exhausting toil. This is not what God had in mind.

Saint John Paul II wrote, "Rest from work is a right." The Bible tells us, "On the seventh day God completed the work he had been doing; he rested on the seventh day from all the work he had undertaken. God blessed the seventh day and made it holy, because on it he rested from all the work he had done in creation" (Gen. 2:2–3).

Sacred Scripture and tradition are two pretty good reasons to recognize that God wants you to take a day off and not let Sunday become Run-day. So, listen to God.

1. Plan ahead. The bottom line is that one should not do work such as errands on Sunday. Do your unpleasant chores on Saturday. Window-shopping and grocery shopping are two different things. Get the milk and eggs stocked up in advance.

2. Power down. Unless you are a trauma surgeon, the world probably does not need to receive your emails and texts. Give yourself a ten-minute window to make sure that there are no emergencies, and then power down.

3. Do what you love. Macramé or macaroni art, museums or martial arts, music or motocross, everyone has his or her delightful thing. Block out some time on Sundays to do what you love.

4. See family and friends. Time goes quickly, and before you know it, your toddler is pledging a fraternity. Call up family and friends and invite them over. The menu is less important than the meal.

5. Pray. God gives us 168 hours in a week, and he asks us to give him one back. The 168 hours are his gift to us; the one hour at Mass is our gift back. Also, take a few minutes before or after Mass to name your blessings and say thanks. Most of the time those blessings will be sitting right next to you in church.

God asks us to rest, to keep holy the Sabbath, because he knew we needed it. What is the point of gaining the whole world and you're too exhausted to enjoy it?

CHAPTER 43

Ways to Use Technology

On YouTube there is an old black-and-white movie of Pope Pius XI opening the Vatican radio station in 1931. A click away is a video of Pope Benedict sending a "tweet" on his iPad. From St. Paul's letters through the Gutenberg printing press until today, the church has embraced technology. In this spirit, I offer you five ways to use technology in a loving and faith-filled way:

1. Press the on/off button. While it is rare to see people use them, all phones and technological gadgets have an off button. This is especially useful when you are sitting down to dinner with your family. Unless you are a trauma surgeon on duty, the world can be deprived of your availability for an hour.

2. Hit mute. Please use it when you dip your fingers in the holy water font at the beginning of Mass.

3. Hit send. You can't talk or email without pushing a send button. Try using it when you are on your mobile phone or reading emails to contact someone you have been thinking about but have not called. It's not just a button; "Send" can be a bridge.

4. Don't forget to save. Even if you don't push save, what you email or say to someone on a text might as well be chiseled in granite for all eternity. So, don't write anything that you would not write on the front page of the *Catholic Standard.*

5. Hit *delete*. When someone sends you an email and asks you to send it to all your friends, please push *delete.* God does not use chain emails, and neither should you.

CHAPTER 44

Get Ready for Heaven

I remember that once I had two funerals in as many days. One was for an older woman, and the other was for a younger man. The first was expected, the second was a tragedy. Both were moments of great grace. For me, a special blessing came from thinking of our Lord's words, "You know neither the day nor the hour" (Matt. 25:13). We may pray for later, but it may be earlier.

Death is inevitable and sad, but it is also the way to heaven. It is not up to us to determine when we will go to meet our Lord, but it is definitely a good idea to be ready. I offer you five dos and don'ts to get ready for heaven:

1. Do expect it. I don't mean to be depressing, but one of these days will be our last. If I live today as if it were the day, I would live it to the fullest. To be aware of death is to live life most completely. It's actually a happy thought. I wouldn't skip my prayers; I would hug the people I love.

2. Don't presume. Yes, you have to die if you want to go to heaven, but some people think that is all there is to it. If that were it, then Jesus' Passion and Resurrection has no meaning. He conquered sin and death on the Cross. His glorious resurrection is the promise to us of eternal joy with him. To take this for granted would be a tragedy. He won the victory, but it is up to me to accept the power of that Cross, to renew myself in my commitment to Jesus each day.

3. Do pray. We can lose touch with old friends. We get busy. After a while we have forgotten to call, and eventually we forget how much we enjoyed the other person's friendship. One day we may bump into them at the grocery store, and the moment will be awkward. Don't do this with Jesus. We should make sure that when we meet Jesus at the pearly gates he says, "Hey, great to see you. I was just talking to you." Jesus doesn't want awkwardness; he just wants joy.

4. Don't get lost. The way to heaven is at once simple and complex. It is simple because Jesus gives us the grace, especially in the sacraments, to find him, know him, love him, and follow him. We just need to place Jesus in the center of our lives. It is complex because life is complex. We have to continually evaluate our priorities to make sure we are on the right path. Just think of the questions Jesus may ask you at the end of your life. The first one may be, Whom did you bring to me?

5. Do pray to St. Joseph. St. Joseph is the patron saint of a happy death. Pray to him that your passing may reflect your life—gentle and calm, with your eyes on Christ and with your heart for the world.

CHAPTER 45

Thing to Do Before the Baby Arrives

Some of my columns come from personal experience, and for some I need to do research. This column definitely fits in the second category. A spiritual father I am, so although I do not have firsthand experience of expecting a child, I have walked with many couples as they await their first child's birth. I canvassed moms and dads alike to bring you top-notch tips on getting ready for the arrival of your amazing blessing. Here are five things to do before the baby arrives:

1. "You shall name him . . ." Mary and Joseph had it easy; the angel Gabriel gave them Jesus' name. Picking a name can be an agonizing process. I have spent sleepless nights trying to name my dogs, but imagine a person! As soon as you come up with a great name, your spouse knew a kid in grammar school who was a bully/nerd/goody-two-shoes, and another name gets struck. That's why the list of saints is a great way of picking out a name for your son or daughter. Give your newborn a real hero as a patron.

2. Make haste. After Mary conceives Jesus, Luke tells us she went in haste to visit her cousin Elizabeth, who was pregnant with John the Baptist. Before Mom may not feel like going out, live a little. Life is about to get busier. Go on a date. As Mary headed out to see her cousin, visit some family and friends.

3. Talk to Joachim and Anne. Tradition names Joachim and Anne as Mary's parents, and therefore Jesus' grandparents. Although there is no biblical record of them, we know she had to have had parents. Also, being a young woman who was open to the Lord, she would certainly have sought the will of the Lord wherever it manifested itself. This most certainly would have included her parents. Joseph, too, would have been open to receiving advice. Expecting moms and dads don't have to know it all, so I recommend talking to your Joachim and Anne for advice. They did a pretty good job with you and would love to know that you value their opinion. In the end it will be your decision, but it is best to have as much input as possible.

4. Give glory to God in the highest. The angels sang this when Jesus our Savior was born. I am pretty sure it is the song that they sing every time a new life enters the world. All life is intended, and God has a plan for every human being. Every child is different, and every child is exceptional in different ways. Remember that "normal" is a cycle on a dishwasher. Love your kid for who she or he is from the very beginning.

5. Be truly present. Prayer is the most important prenatal care. It not only helps the baby but helps new moms and dads alleviate stress, realize blessings, and receive strength for the challenges of parenthood. The Mass is the most perfect prayer, so make sure you never miss it. Know why? Jesus is truly present in the Eucharist, and each time mom receives Communion, the baby spends extra-special personal time, up close, with him. Imagine mom, dad, and baby spending a little quiet time after Mass in the Real Presence of the Lord of life!

CHAPTER 46

Ways to Get to the Top

Growing in holiness is kind of like climbing a mountain. However, instead of struggling to the top on our own, we actually get to the top by letting go of the mountain and allowing Jesus to carry us up. He died on the Cross so that we could be saved. As the first letter of Peter puts it, "For Christ also suffered for sins once, the righteous for the sake of the unrighteous, that he might lead you to God. Put to death in the flesh, he was brought to life in the spirit" (1 Pet. 3:18). He does the lifting; we just have to be lifted. Not always as easy as it seems.

Through our Baptism, we are in Jesus' arms, but we need to cooperate as he ascends the steep slopes. Think of holding a toddler. If they want down, it is almost impossible to carry them. We don't want to be the cross; we want to help carry the cross. With this in mind, I offer five ways to get to the top with Jesus:

1. Exercise the good muscle. Imagine virtue as a muscle in your body. Every time you do something good, your virtue muscles grow stronger. However, if we don't exercise regularly, our muscles can atrophy and shrivel up. Be conscious of working out virtue in your life. Always be asking yourself, "Is this making me stronger in faith and love?" Go for strength.

2. Weakness is good. St. Paul says that the Lord told him, "My grace is sufficient for you, for power is made perfect in weakness" (2 Cor. 12:9). We have to recognize that the Lord's strength in us makes us good. His love makes my love perfect. His courage gives me the boldness to proclaim the gospel. His forgiveness of me allows me to show true mercy to others.

3. Take just one cookie. When a fat person eats a cookie, they might say, "I might as well eat the whole bag." When a skinny person eats a cookie, they may say, "I need to work out a little more tomorrow." To get to the top, we need to break a cycle of failure that causes us to throw in the towel when we should be doing deep knee bends to pick it up. Willpower rarely sustains us, so ask for God's help to do the right thing. Seriously, just ask God, "Please help me to do the right thing." God will listen. You must too.

4. Pray before the lights go out. Socrates said, "The unexamined life is not worth living." To stop and take stock is a key element of following the Lord. Before the lights go out at bedtime, thank God for the gift of the day. Ask the Lord for the blessing to know him and follow him more closely. Then replay the day. Look for times when you noticed him, when you ignored him, when you avoided him, when you welcomed him. Finally, make a plan for the next day.

5. Take it personally. Christianity is about knowing, loving, and following the risen Christ. It's personal because we follow and love a person whom we can meet in his humanity and by his divine nature be brought into the very life of God. We come to know and love him in Scripture and the sacraments—especially in the Eucharist. This means that when we spend time with Scripture and in church before the tabernacle, we can be as present to him as he is to us at each moment of our lives. We learn to love him by how he loves us.

CHAPTER 47

Baseball Is Good for Your Family

The Washington Nationals' stadium sits in my parish. On a summer night, I can sit in my backyard and hear the roar of the crowd. Being just blocks from the Capitol, we also have our fair share of Republicans and Democrats. They may not agree on much, but my "reds" and "blues" all have a penchant for the 'Nats.

There seems to be less and less that parents can let their children watch or surf, but baseball is still safe. Not only is it safe, I contend that baseball is good for the family. Here are five reasons why I think this is true:

1. Try again. Baseball has 162 games in a regular season. If you lose one, just wait until tomorrow when there will be a whole other chance to win again. In life it would be sad if you defined success or failure by one single event. If your family hits a roadblock, pick yourselves up, get the help you need, and play for the full season, not just the day.

2. No time frame. Baseball does not have a time clock. A game can be short or long. You never know. Life is the same way. Don't sweat the small stuff. Cherish your loved ones, and live and forgive each day fully

3. A lot of threes. God, who is three persons in one God, must love baseball. Three strikes, three outs, nine (a multiple of three) innings. The Father, Son, and Holy Spirit are the realest reality there is. Each of these three persons are part of a community of diversity. There are tons of implications of this. One is that if the people you love do things differently than you, it is not necessarily a bad thing.

4. Sacrifice and teamwork. In order for one player to score, another player may sacrifice a hit with a fly or bunt. Baseball is a team sport. You may be the best outfielder, but you also need the other guy catching your throw to be good. Relationship with others is about working together. Sacrifice and teamwork are part of that plan.

5. Count the blessings. Ted Williams, the great Boston Red Sox left fielder, once said, "Baseball is the only field of endeavor where a man can succeed three times out of ten and be considered a good performer." I am not advocating for a seventy-percent failure rate in families but rather a different scoreboard. Instead of counting flubs, count the blessings.

CHAPTER 48

Great Disciples to Inspire

Women of faith have developed some of the most important infrastructure in our land. Religious sisters established hospital networks and were the founders of our parochial school system. Catholic women have been a voice defending those who have no voice. These strong women served the poor, greeted the immigrant, and educated generations of children.

A prayer of gratitude must be offered for all those whose strength and love have formed our world and, more importantly, our church. Here are but five of my many female heroes who are amazing examples of discipleship:

1. Catherine of Siena. This fourteenth-century Third Order Dominican sister was a mystic, author, and servant of the poor. What I admire most about her is her capacity to speak truth to power. During this period the popes had abandoned Rome and were living in Avignon, France. This little sister convinced Gregory XI that the papacy need to return to Rome, the place where St. Peter lived and died as the first pope. Catholic women have always been known for *chutzpah*.

2. Dorothy Day. A convert to Catholicism, Dorothy Day had lived a "bohemian" lifestyle before finding faith. She knew the world and embraced Christ instead. She was a social activist and cofounder of the Catholic Worker Movement, which sought through nonviolence to defend and care for the poor and homeless. One of my favorite things about Dorothy is that she was arrested many times advocating for the poor. She had guts and grace all rolled into one. Her autobiography *The Long Loneliness* is a wonderful spiritual read.

3. Mother Teresa. We all know how amazing Mother Teresa was. I met her once and was struck by the fact that she was so short. St. Teresa is a reminder that God's power working through us does not require stature or size, just a desire to do his will above all else.

4. My mom. (She's going to be mad that I included her on this list, but it's my list so I can put anybody I want on it.) Mary Byrne is mom of eight, grandmother of twenty-two, and great-grandmother of thirteen, and everyone gets a Christmas gift, including our dogs. At ninety-seven she is a daily communicant and brings Communion to scores of people who are decade younger than she is. She treats the executive and the janitor with the same dignity and grace. Mom is a continual reminder that being a believer and having a smile go together.

5. The Blessed Mother. No list of disciples would be complete without the very first disciple. Mary said yes to God from her conception to the foot of the Cross. Her acceptance of God's will made salvation possible, and she reminds us that each day we, too, must bring Jesus into our wounded world.

CHAPTER 49

Understanding Forgiveness

"Father, forgive them, for they know not what they do" (Luke 23:34). These are among the last words that Jesus spoke. As he endures the greatest suffering imaginable, he prays for those who inflict his pain. It makes sense that one petition of the Lord's Prayer says, "Forgive us our trespasses as we forgive those who trespass against us." Forgiveness is essential for being his disciple, and often it can be the hardest part of following him. Heaven is a no-grudge zone, so here are five ways to understand forgiveness:

1. His gift. All good things are from God. Forgiveness is not a psychological process; it is a spiritual one. Don't be too proud to beg for the gift to forgive someone. How does

God forgive all? Because he understands all. Pray for the gift of wisdom.

2. Not amnesia. Remember that forgiving someone does not erase the sting of a painful memory. Forgiveness does not make a painful memory happy, but it provides a new context.

3. My burden. Your grudge is your burden, not someone else's. This is especially true if you have no contact with the person whom you need to forgive, particularly if the person is dead. Remember that carrying this burden means we are allowing someone else's sin to remain active in our lives. Address the evil spirit of that sin, and banish it from your life. This is usually not a one-and-done exercise. Continue each time it sneaks up and tries to lure you away from him. The way of forgiveness is the way of freedom.

4. Rewrite the story. One of the reasons we can hold onto the burden of unforgiveness is that we have told the story in only one way. The narrative usually focuses on the bad that happened to me. In prayer, retell the story, emphasizing the graces that God poured into the situation—the strength, the courage, and the fortitude he gave you. You survived and maybe even grew wiser. This is the new memory. Pray to notice his virtue, not dwell on another's vice.

5. At the foot of the Cross. At the foot of the Cross, we experience the transformative power of mercy. Jesus has taken *my* sins, *my* anger, *my* unforgiveness and nailed them to the Cross. He has taken even death itself, upon himself, *for me.* In the Resurrection, Jesus transforms my sins by his love for *me.* In the shadow of that Cross, as I look upon him who cries out for my forgiveness, how can I but not forgive those who have trespassed against me?

CHAPTER 50

Things I Learned from My Puppy

It seems fitting that I began this book with a nod to one of my old friends, and I end it with an introduction to my new friend. I got a puppy. Her name is Zélie after St. Zélie Martin, the mother of St. Thérèse of Lisieux. Pope Francis declared Zélie and her husband, Louis, saints. They are the first married couple ever canonized together.

Although having an adorable destruction machine is a lot of work, it is also tons of fun, not just for me but also for the school kids and the whole parish as well. As a new papa, I offer five things I have learned from my puppy:

1. Mouthy. Puppies explore the world with their mouths. From socks to sticks, they want to put everything in their mouths. It's my job to make sure she only gets her mouth on the right stuff. It reminds me that everything in the fridge—the donuts after Mass, the treats that people drop off at the rectory—need not end up in my mouth. God gave me the gift of temperance, the virtue that helps me say no to earthly pleasure so as to enjoy them in moderation. Next time I am at the buffet, I just need to remember that I am not a puppy.

2. Schedules are good. In order to get a puppy rectory-trained, one needs two things: a schedule and a crate. Puppies don't pee where they sleep, so if you keep them on a good schedule and let them nap in their crates, they pick up pretty quickly that the privy is outside. An interesting side effect of this process is that it keeps me on a schedule too. The morning walk is not an option now, and its timing must be regular. Funny how God can use anything to bring us blessings.

3. Not just friends. Zélie doesn't need me to be just a friend; I have to also be the one who leads her to make good decisions. This reminds me of our beloved former archbishop Cardinal Hickey's episcopal motto *veritatem in caritate* (truth in love). We need to love people enough to tell them the truth. Whatever we say, we must always say it with love.

4. Positive is better. The days of smacking the dog are gone. It doesn't work. They don't truly understand, and that kind of discipline just makes the puppy afraid of you. Dogs learn to do the good because they are praised for it. Bad stuff is made unpleasant, but the real benefit comes from positivity. This is how God works with us. When we had sinned, he sent his Son to save us not condemn us. Not a bad lesson for life. Praise the positive and show mercy to the sinner.

5. At his heals. Zélie follows me around. I am her pack leader, and where I am is the best and safest place to be. I need to always remember that Jesus is my pack leader. I need to make sure I am always in his presence because it is the best and safest place to be.

Acknowledgments

I am most grateful to Mark Zimmerman for urging me to write these thoughts and Mark Shriver for hounding me to make them a book. Thank you to Nena Madonia Oshman of Dupree Miller & Associates for helping me to partner with Loyola Press and Gary Jansen for his insightful edits. Lastly, light and love to Roma Downey for writing the foreword.

About the Author

Fr. William (Bill) Byrne is a native of Washington, D.C., and is currently the pastor of Our Lady of Mercy Parish in Potomac, Maryland. He has taught at the North American College in Rome and has spoken at numerous conferences in the United States. In 2016, Pope Francis named Fr. Byrne a Missionary of Mercy for the Jubilee Year of Mercy. His dog Zélie credits herself as the muse for his writing.